# STICKS AND STONES

Emotional Abuse and Verbal Attacks

Through Lies, Vows, Curses, and Judgments

Help from a Christian Perspective

Dr. Lynda L. Irons

Irons Quill

Dr. Lynda L. Irons

Cover by H. Gene Irons

Scripture taken from the NEW AMERICAN STANDARD BIBLE, Copyright © 1960, 1962, 1963, 1968, 1971, 1972, 1973, 1975, 1977, 1995 by The Lockman Foundation. Used by permission.

All rights reserved. Except for brief quotes no portion of this book may be reproduced, stored in a retrieval system, or transmitted in any form – electronic, mechanical, photocopy, recording, scanning, or other means without prior approval from and/or crediting this author. Contact Dr. Lynda L. Irons at ironsquillreader@gmail.com.

# TABLE OF CONTENTS

| | | Page |
|---|---|---|
| | Introduction | 4 |
| 1. | Lies | 13 |
| 2. | Vows | 25 |
| 3. | Curses | 35 |
| 4. | Judgments | 49 |
| 5. | Effects of Verbal Assaults | 65 |
| 6. | Listening for Verbal Assaults | 78 |
| 7. | Release from Verbal Assaults | 116 |
| 8. | Emotions and Beliefs | 125 |
| 9. | Blessings | 140 |
| 10. | Sample Prayers | 145 |
| 11. | From Verbal Assault to Truth | 162 |
| 12. | Weapons of Warfare | 173 |
| | Concluding Remarks | 182 |
| | Books by this author | 184 |

Dr. Lynda L. Irons

# INTRODUCTION

Nearly every child has said, "Sticks and stones may break my bones, but words will never hurt me." Or "I'm rubber, you're glue. Everything you say bounces off of me and sticks to you." A young Solomon might have said, "A curse without a cause shall not alight." But we all know that words hurt. Most children would rather be physically beaten than endure a demeaning tongue-lashing tirade. It is a rare person who has never been subjected to emotional abuse and verbal attacks on some level.

In this day and age, we hear of school shootings and suicides. Bullying, most often verbal assaults, are found to be the basis for such drastic measures. According to the CDC, suicide is the third leading cause of death among young people, resulting in over four thousand deaths per year. According to Yale University studies, bullying victims are between two and nine times more likely to consider suicide than non-victims. Words hurt.

Verbal assaults and the consequences of embracing them have caused problems for everyone from the youngest to the oldest and from the uneducated to the highly educated. They affect males and females in all walks of life. They plague believers and unbelievers without partiality.

Too many people find themselves stuck in a rut. They may describe their actions with the words, "I constantly shoot myself in the foot." Or, "I continually run into a wall." Or, "I keep circling the same old mountain." They desire to grow and mature, but seem to be held back by some unseen, yet very real, obstacle. The root of the problem is very often some verbal assault that sounds true, feels true, and seems logical because of tangible evidence that appears to support it.

Any lie, vow, curse, or judgment can be a verbal assault. A verbal assault is like a two-edged sword, that is, it can cause injury to the one who speaks it as well as to the one to whom it is spoken. Verbally attacking someone else, or being verbally abused by someone else, will have negative effects upon the body, the soul, the spirit, emotions, behavior, attitudes, and more. Those effects range from mild to severe on the abuse continuum.

Some verbal assaults are disguised in statements of expectation or instruction. Depending upon the way it is processed, it can have far reaching effects in the life of the one who embraces it. For example, a married man with several children was still feeling the pain of his father's rejections. He processed his father's neglectfulness and criticisms by embracing the thoughts, "I do not have much worth." "I was never good enough." "I can't accomplish anything." "I lived up to his expectation of failure." He astutely observed, "Whenever I get close to success, I sabotage it."

There were implied vows hidden within those observations. Those implied vows locked him into failure. There were lies which fed distressing emotions. His father's curses and judgments compounded his pain and generated even more negative thoughts and emotions. Both he and his wife were weary of the cycles of hope and despair as he subconsciously sabotaged any career successes. Once he recognized his father's statements for what they were, he was able to take authority over them and begin to reverse the cycles of failure and despair.

It is fairly easy to relate to other believers who go through cycle after cycle of apparent victory only to be plunged back into the same old thoughts, attitudes, and behaviors. Who has not agonized in prayer without successfully addressing the root of the problem? The cyclical living will often include addictions and other harmful behavior. (See list of books by this author for more details on cutting, eating disorders, anger issues, and more.)

The impact of verbal assaults is felt from an early age. Many instinctively resisted or defied them as children. Others were so inundated by a constant flow of criticisms, insults, judgments, gossip, slander, and so on, that they surrendered to the onslaught. Perhaps whatever was spoken was embraced because it came from someone in authority such as a parent, clergy member, or teacher. Maybe it came from people who were bigger, older, stronger, or out-numbered the target.

Circumstances seemed to have reinforced the "truth" of those words. They were then further embedded into the person's life. Recurrences of the same kinds of issues are noted, compelling one to ask, "Why do I always seem to run into this kind of person or that kind of situation?" "Do I have a 'loser' sign on my forehead?" Or, the observation may come, "I've always been like this. I've always had this problem." One young woman said, "Hey, it's the same song, just a different verse."

This phenomenon is more than just a coincidence and we will explore the reasons for these things in a later chapter. Joy Dawson said in <u>Intimate Friendship with God</u>, "If we are bombarded continually in any one area of our Christian life with satanic attacks, we will know demonic spirits have been listening to what is coming out of our mouths or they have been observing what we are doing." I would add that they also observe what has been done to us.

The good news is that we are not doomed to continue to repeat cycles of defeat. Sin, including verbal assaults, generates strongholds. Demons operate out of the strongholds. Unfortunately, most of us have not benefited from teaching about these matters, so we suffer from the effects of sin, strongholds, and demonic oppression for too many years or decades.

Satan is a liar. There is just enough reasonableness and "truth" in his deceptions that we can be misled. A high school girl was told by her guidance counselor, "You're not college material. You should get your diploma and get the highest paying factory job you can find." The girl looked at her less than stellar grade point average. The evidence was there. However, she was a fighter and a few years later, she worked up the courage to try one college class. She aced it. She then began to believe that she was not destined to be a factory worker. In fact, after her first year of college, she had a 3.8 grade point average. The truth was that her brain needed a little more time to develop, her soul needed more encouragement, and her spirit needed the maturity to rely upon God.

Demons can imitate us so that we think that the thoughts are our own. Demons can introduce thoughts into our minds. This is not a very comfortable concept for any believer. Satan put thoughts into David's mind in 1 Chronicles 21:1. It says that Satan stood up against Israel and moved, provoked, incited, stirred up, made David number the people. Peter addressed Ananias. *Ananias, why has Satan filled your heart to lie to the Holy Spirit?* Acts 5:3.

David was a man after God's own heart. Ananias was probably present at Pentecost. These were Spirit-filled men. If it could happen to them, why would any believer be immune? It is disconcerting to think of being influenced by a demon, but *if* this is the source of the problem and this possibility is ignored, the enemy will be able to continue to deceive and oppress from the vantage point of that stronghold.

People are created in the image of God. God spoke things into existence. While we do not create something out of nothing, things can be spoken into existence. Proverbs 23:7 says that as a man thinks or reckons in his soul or heart, so he is. If you reckon that you are destined to be factory worker, you will likely be a factory worker. If you think you are college material, you will achieve success there. Thoughts and words affect behavior, emotions, and attitudes. Believing a deception has the same effect as believing the truth. Thoughts, feelings, and actions will line up according to whatever "truth" is accepted.

Examine and guard thoughts and words without becoming semi-superstitious about every word. There are some people who believe that they are cursing themselves by stating, "I have diabetes." or "I have a cold." How do we pray for the sick if no one acknowledges that they are sick? Jesus never told someone to deny their sicknesses. He welcomed them so they could be healed.

Consider also that words constitute only about seven to ten percent of our communication. The tone of spoken words is about thirty-five to thirty-eight percent. Body language, though unspoken, can articulate volumes. Facial expressions, especially the eyes, can also convey much – fifty to fifty-five percent according to Milton H. Erickson. People have said, "If looks could kill, I'd be dead."

Margaret Thatcher warned:
Watch your thoughts, they become words.
Watch your words, they become actions.
Watch your actions, they become habits.
Watch your habits, they become character.
Watch your character, it becomes your destiny.

Chuck Swindoll said, "Thoughts: they either control you, or you control them. Dr. Myles Munroe said, "A thought is a silent word. Therefore, a word is an exposed thought." Jesus said, *"I say to you, that every careless word that people speak, they shall give an accounting for it in the day of judgment. For by your words you will be justified, and by your words you will be condemned."* Matthew 12:36, 37.

The Bible has much to say about our communication. Take the time to do a study on the many verses that address thoughts and words, the things that go through the mind as well as speculations, and knowledge and truth. *And do not be conformed to this world, but be transformed by the renewing of your mind, so that you may prove what the will of God is, that which is good and acceptable and perfect.* Romans 12:2. *We are destroying speculations and every lofty thing raised up against the knowledge of God, and we are taking every thought captive to the obedience of Christ.* 2 Corinthians 10:5.

How does one move from embracing a painful "truth" to embracing the Truth of the Word of God? How does one get freed from a vow when it is not recognized or even remembered? What will bring release from curses and judgments? It is not simply a matter of denying them, gutting it out, or repeating Scripture verses over and over again, or we would have moved on by now. Those deep, old messages which have pierced to the core of a person can echo painfully for years.

We will look at four common categories of verbal assaults, use the weapons we have been given to tear down strongholds, and rebuke demonic oppressors. We will learn to replace those things of the enemy's kingdom with the goodness of the Kingdom of God. Release from verbal assaults will come with the recognition of their existence, applying Scriptural principles, and using the sample prayers and other tools to bring freedom from frustrating cycles of failure.

# 1
# LIES

"If I'm in a crowd of people, I will get hurt and be in trouble." This statement felt true to this middle-aged man. Indeed, he was hurt as a child in group settings. As an adult he continued to avoid crowds. His fears confined him to his home more often than not. When he came for prayer about his agoraphobia issues, the Lord brought him to a couple of memories. One occurred on a playground. In this event he was bullied and teased. Another memory was of a church camp in which he was picked on and physically injured during one of the more rowdy games. As a child, he interpreted these events by embracing the notion that crowds were perilous to his well-being. Because no one helped him process the events at the time, he believed the lies and spent a lonely life avoiding crowds.

For purposes of brevity, I will most often use the word, "lie". Bear in mind that lies also encompass deceptions, misinterpretations, and faulty processing, as well as the fuller meanings given in the original Greek and Hebrew languages. One familiar Greek word is *pseudo*. There are several American words with that prefix such as pseudonym which means a false or fictitious name, a pen name.

Other Greek and Hebrew words mean falsehood, lie, pretend, unreal, deception, guile, deceptive character, treacherous dealing, false dealing, and other activities and words that define a way of life that goes contrary to the Law of God.

Most people tend to dismiss the spiritual impact of violating the laws and principles of the Word of God which tells us not to bear false witness. A lie is more than just telling a fib. A so-called white lie is not harmless. Lying by omission is destructive as well. Self-deception is also a terrible curse. By embracing self-deception we add agreement to our ignorance. There are too many wounded people who do not fully understand what a lie is and so there is an inability to appreciate how deeply it can influence a life. Consider also that embracing lies may also taint future generations.

As previously stated, any sin – whether committed by or against a person – will create a stronghold in the spiritual realm. That stronghold is where demons gain their so-called legal right to oppress, plague, or torment. They will continue to do so until they are intentionally rebuked after demolishing the stronghold that was established by the sin of the lie.

The following biblical examples illustrate the power of believing lies or truth. Remember, there is often an element of truth hidden within a lie or deception which confuses or baits the targeted person. This is where faith enters in. There must be an intentional choice to believe what God says in His Word or else the natural situation will dictate what is believed.

Some people refuse to accept truth. They prefer to live in denial. If someone refuses to face the reality of their situation, there is little that will help them. They are destined to repeat cycles of frustration and defeat. Those who care for and love a person like this will also be affected. As a counselor, I could instruct and pray for someone, but I could not want freedom for the counselee more than he or she wanted it for him or herself.

It is also a matter of jurisdiction. We cannot impose our desires upon another. The affected person must take ownership of his or her own issues. If help is sought, that is the time to step in and prayerfully help.

## Dr. Lynda L. Irons

Spiritual reality is superior to natural reality. Pierre Chardin astutely said, "We are not humans having a spiritual experience; we are spirits having a human experience." Vance Havner said, "If you are a Christian, you are not a citizen of this world trying to get to heaven; you are a citizen of heaven making your way through this world." We so often lose sight of this profound truth.

In the following examples, the people who saw spiritual reality responded with courage and boldness in their circumstances. Those who only saw through their natural eyes lived under fear and made assumptions about reality. They misinterpreted the situation and used faulty processing to come to their conclusions. Their conclusions directed their actions and fueled their negative emotions.

Deuteronomy 1:1 – 33 and Numbers 13:30 – 14:28 record the account of Israel at Kadesh-barnea. God had just delivered them from Egypt. The Egyptians were drowned in the sea, they had received the Law, and they traveled eleven days to the edge of the Promised Land. They sent twelve men to spy out the land. All of them agreed that the land was wonderful, but it was filled with strong people and fortified cities.

# Sticks and Stones

Ten of the men said that the land devours its inhabitants and all the people in it were men of great size. They concluded, *we became like grasshoppers in our own sight, and so we were in their sight.* They further processed the situation by embracing the thoughts that God hated them and wanted to kill them, that their wives and children would be plundered and that it would better to be back in Egypt. Those lies and deceptions were believed because they were seeing with physical eyes only. There was truth in what they perceived, but they believed the natural evidence rather than God's promises. They lacked faith.

Two men, Joshua and Caleb, reminded the Israelites of God's promises to bring them into the land which flows with milk and honey. They exhorted them not to rebel against the Lord or to be afraid of the inhabitants of the land because God was with them and would remove the protection from their enemies. These men of faith saw the situation with spiritual eyes and believed God's reality.

The people chose to believe the lies of the ten spies rather than the promises of God as expressed through Joshua and Caleb. The people threatened to stone them and return to Egypt. Fear drove their attitudes and behaviors. God responded to their lack of faith with one of the most frightening pronouncements in Scripture. *Say to them, "As I* live," says the LORD, "just as you have spoken in My hearing, so I will surely do to you ..." Numbers 14:28. And He did.

Seeing with natural eyes rather than spiritual eyes cost the ten spies their lives. Their entire generation would not enter the Promised Land. Furthermore, their children would suffer consequences of their doubts and unfaithfulness by wandering in the wilderness for an additional forty years until that generation died.

Observe the differences in the emotions of the two groups. The majority felt fear, turmoil, anger, confusion, suspicion, rebelliousness, and distrust. The minority felt confidence in God. They were bold, courageous, excited, and trusting. What a contrast between the slave mentality of the majority and the warrior mentality of the few!

2 Kings 6:14-17 is another passage that illustrates the contrast between physical and spiritual realities, fear and faith, lies and truth. The prophet Elisha was in a city that was surrounded by an enemy army. They wanted to kill him. Gehazi, his servant, saw the army and was terrified. Elisha saw the spiritual reality. He prayed, *"O LORD, I pray, open his eyes that he may see."* When the Lord opened the servant's eyes, he was also able to perceive the spiritual reality: the mountain was full of horses and chariots of fire that had been sent to protect Elisha.

## Sticks and Stones

He went from fearful to confident, from lies to truth, in that instant.

1 Samuel 17:28 - 37 is the account of a young David refusing to accept the lies, curses, and judgments of his older brother, Eliab. This occurred just prior to David volunteering to fight the giant, Goliath. If he would have embraced the things his brother said, he would likely have just dropped off the cheese, gotten a report for his father, and gone back to tending his sheep. Instead, he countered the accusations with truth and killed a giant.

Eliab, his oldest brother asked him, *"Why have you come down? What did you do with your few sheep?"* He judged and belittled David. *"I know your insolence and the wickedness of your heart. You just came to see the battle."* He also cursed/judged David by saying, *"You are not able to go against this Philistine to fight with him, you are but a youth while he has been a warrior from his youth."* There was an element of truth in what he said, but David did not yield to the verbal assaults.

David countered with the truth - *"The LORD who delivered me from the paw of the lion and from the paw of the bear, He will deliver me from the hand of this Philistine."* David refused to receive or believe the lies, curses, and judgments of his older brother. David chose to believe the truth that God had protected him in the past and would continue to do so. David was already anointed to be the king and believed that God would fulfill His word. No bear or brother, lion or giant, would stand in the way!

Jesus had a conversation with the Pharisees in John 8:32, 33. He said, *"You shall know the truth and the truth shall make you free. They answered Him, 'We are Abraham's offspring, and have never yet been enslaved to anyone; how is it that You say, "You shall become free?"'"* It is astounding to think that these Pharisees were faced every day with Roman soldiers. Surely they remembered their history of being taken into captivity by the Babylonians. How could they have forgotten Moses and the four hundred years of slavery in Egypt?

In Mark 4:37 - 41 we see the example of the disciples believing some very subtle lies. They were in the sea when a storm came up. Jesus was sleeping. They woke Him and said, *"Teacher, do You not care that we are perishing?"* This must have been a very severe storm because several of the disciples were seasoned fishermen.

If the question they asked was to be transposed into a statement, it would clarify the subtle lies. The statement would be, "Teacher, You do not care that we are going to perish." There are three subtle lies – He is merely a teacher, that is, He is not the miracle-working Savior of the world. Another subtle implication is that He does not care. The third lie is that they would surely die. They were filled with fear and doubt.

In spite of the signs and miracles they had already witnessed, they believed that He could not save them. In spite of the many times they saw Jesus' compassion on multitudes, they implied that He did not care about them. These thoughts came from young men who experienced this life-threatening storm near the beginning of Jesus' ministry. Their faith had not yet matured.

Acts 27 illustrates a contrast to this. The apostle Paul endured a life-threatening storm and subsequent shipwreck. He believed God who told him that he would live to testify in Rome. *Do not be afraid, Paul, you must stand before Caesar; and behold, God has granted you all those who are sailing with you.* Acts 27:24.

What was the difference? Paul was mature in his faith. He'd been delivered from much affliction. He received the promises of God and believed that he would make it to Rome. He may have been alarmed about the circumstances, but he was confident in the Lord.

The above Biblical examples clearly demonstrate the relationship between beliefs and feelings, thoughts and emotions. **If what is believed is not based on truth, then what is felt will not match**

**reality.** There is a distinct choice between belief in the reality of what the inferior natural senses detect and the belief in what the superior spiritual senses and faith in God express about a greater reality.

A little girl was marked by an obvious physical defect. Because of that deformity and other things, she was ridiculed, shamed, humiliated, embarrassed, made fun of, and laughed at by family, peers, and teachers to the point that she eventually dropped out of high school. As an adult she truly believed, "I'm unworthy of anything good." "I don't deserve happiness."

We asked the Holy Spirit to take us to the root of these thoughts. She immediately came to a memory of being about four years old. Her father had set off some fireworks. As she excitedly ran to a rocking chair the wind caught her dress and lifted it. Her father yelled at her and said, "I saw your butt." She processed this by concluding, "It is not okay for me to be happy and excited."

I suggested that we revisit that memory and invite Jesus to minister to her there. I told her that she may "see" Him with her spiritual eyes, "hear" Him with her spiritual ears, sense His presence in the memory, or realize truth. As she quieted herself and focused on the memory, Jesus ministered to her. She said, "I can only see Daddy now and a heavy weight being lifted. I feel warmth flooding me. It's okay to be happy."

We went to several other memories in which she was humiliated. She forgave the offenders and received more peace and freedom. The wonderful thing about Jesus bringing truth in one situation is that His truth extends to every place in which that specific lie has been embedded. Truth has a ripple effect. She later reported that there were more ripples of healing from past memories as well as in current relationships.

A young teen accidentally cut her arm. Her mother wrapped the deep gash in towels. Her father did not think that she needed stitches. As she became light-headed from the loss of blood, she processed the situation by thinking, "They won't miss me if I die; they have a bunch of other kids." Later when they dropped her off at a clinic, she received immediate attention from the staff. She interpreted it with the thoughts, "These strangers care more about me than my family does." "I can't trust my family to take care of me, so I'll have to take care of myself." Is it any wonder that she felt estranged from her family and seldom asked for help with problems?

The people in the examples repeated the thoughts and words as well as the actions that were driven by them. They reinforced the lie, deception, faulty processing, and/or misinterpretation. They locked their responses in with vows. They sowed them like dandelions, breathed on the puffball, and ended up with a field of weeds that choked out the flowers.

It comes down to belief in the truth of God and His Word. Bill Johnson says in <u>When Heaven Invades Earth</u>, that if there are misconceptions regarding who God is and what He is like, faith will be limited. Belief is assurance in what is evident in the spiritual realm. Unbelief is faith in the inferior natural realm. I value the words of Neil Anderson and Rich Miller from <u>Getting Anger Under Control</u>: "If what we believe does not conform to truth, then what we feel does not conform to reality."

# 2
# VOWS

𝔄 teacher suffered a heart attack and suddenly died during the high school assembly. The shaken students were rushed to their first period classes. The teacher in one class callously said, "Life goes on, turn to chapter ten in your book." A sensitive young teen processed this trauma in a poem that he entitled "The Day After I Die." In the poem there were a number of overt and subtle vows relating to blocking the grief and moving on to the next thing. The immediate unintended consequence was that he was unable to grieve the death of that teacher. The subsequent consequence was that he could not grieve the deaths of his parents or best friend decades later as an adult.

He sought help for depression and this memory was one to which the Lord brought him. He renounced the entire poem and gave the Lord the opportunity to then replace the callous fence that he had built around his heart with freedom to face the grief. He gave himself permission to grieve the losses. The next time he went to the cemetery where his parents were buried, he spontaneously released the deeply buried grief with a flood of tears.

Vows can be good things or bad things; they can have negative or positive effects. An example of a positive vow would be a marriage vow. Another is the vow of a physician who pledged that she would do whatever was necessary to get to the root of her patient's problem. Another example of a negative vow would be like the one a vengeful young man voiced. "I have to make people pay. I have to make myself pay." He spent a lifetime of alienating himself from others for real or imagined, small or large offenses. He sabotaged himself by ruining any success he had in relationships, education, and career. His vow also had the unintentional consequence of extending to his relationship with God.

Vows tend to be one of the primary reasons that people become stuck in a rut. Usually the vows have their roots in childhood as a response to a difficult or traumatic situation. These are often forgotten, but they will continue to bind the one who makes the vows to those vows and keep the fences in place. The vow-maker will then continue to run in circles or shoot himself in the foot or circle that same mountain until each vow is dealt with in a biblical manner.

Our modern-day concept of a vow corresponds more to a promise, a pledge, or a commitment. They are generally not thought of as being serious or binding. The meanings of the biblical Greek and Hebrew words are much stronger than our American definitions.

The Hebrew word means, among other things, to bind your soul with an oath. The Greek word is equivalent to a fence, an enclosure, that which restrains. Vows are not outgrown with age. They do not evaporate. This is why a vow made earlier in life can keep someone bound or running into that invisible fence.

John and Paula Sandford state in <u>The Transformation of the Inner Man</u>, "An inner vow is a determination set by the mind and heart into the being early in life… as children; usually forgotten. Our inner being persistently retains such programming no matter what changes of mind and heart may later pertain. The distinctive mark of an inner vow is that it resists the normal maturation process."

John and Stasi Eldredge say in their book, <u>Captivating</u>, "The vows we make as children are very understandable – and very, very damaging.

They shut our hearts down. They are essentially a deep-seated agreement with the messages of our wounds. They act as an agreement with the verdict on us."

Vows that cause problems are often made in response to an actual or perceived threat or to a deep emotional wound. They serve as self-protection. A vow is generally intended to apply to one specific situation or person. Unfortunately, there are unintended consequences that usually become a part of the equation as in the example of the teen who could not grieve appropriately.

That hurtful situation or relationship from which one attempts to protect him or herself often involves sin of some kind that compels the declaration, "I will never forgive her." Or, "If he does that one more time, I will pay him back." This would constitute sin in response to the other person's real or perceived sin. That response-sin will compound negative effects in life by creating strongholds from which the enemy can oppress the one who made the vow.

Yes. Be angry. There has been an injustice. The emotion is not a sin. What is done with it may or may not be a sin. The Bible admonishes us to be angry and *not* sin for our own sakes so that we can remain free.

## Sticks and Stones

So then, the initial insult, offense, or assault may create a stronghold. A sinful response to that initial issue creates another stronghold. Any vows or deceptions or faulty processing become the source of yet another stronghold. Each stronghold becomes the potential launching pad for the enemy's oppressive arrows.

A young teen did not realize that she made a vow when her best friend died: "I won't have friends anymore because they just die." This was a vow. Unintended consequences caused unexpected repercussions. She did not really intend to never have any friends ever again, but the fence she built with her vow made it very difficult to make and maintain friendships even into her adult years. She did not intend for it to apply to her relationship with God either, but that was yet another consequence.

A vow was made. A fence was built. A soul was bound. A stronghold was then established. Because Satan is a legalist, he preys on such opportunities to extend the vow to apply in a much broader sense than it was intended. This seems especially true of childhood vows that may be easily forgotten or not recognized as a vow. They must be dealt with intentionally using biblical principles.

Yes, born-again, Spirit-filled Christian believers can be oppressed (not possessed) by the enemy.

Again, ask David, a man after God's own heart. *Then Satan stood up against Israel and moved David to number Israel.* 1 Chronicles 21:1. Ask Ananias and Sapphira, who were likely at Pentecost. *But Peter said, "Ananias, why has Satan filled your heart to lie to the Holy Spirit, and to keep back some of the price of the land?"* Acts 5:3. Ask Paul, who wrote much of the New Testament. *And because of the surpassing greatness of the revelations, for this reason, to keep me from exalting myself, there was given me a thorn in the flesh, a messenger of Satan to buffet me – to keep me from exalting myself!* 2 Corinthians 12:7. *For we wanted to come to you – I, Paul, more than once – and yet Satan thwarted us.* 1 Thessalonians 2:18.

Note: The Greek New Testament word, *daimonizomai*, is more accurately translated "demonized." For an unbeliever, it would mean that the person acts under the influence of the demon and may well be possessed by that demon. For a believer who is indwelt by the Holy Spirit, it would mean that he or she was oppressed, thwarted, buffeted, and so on, that is, pressured from the outside.

Again, it is not very comfortable to think about being influenced by a demon, but *if* this is the source of the problem and this possibility is ignored, the enemy will be able to continue to oppress from that stronghold. God looks at the heart. Satan does not. Satan is a legalist and a squatter. Until and unless the vow is rendered null and void, the stronghold is demolished, and the enemy is rebuked in the name of Jesus, he will continue to oppress.

Many vows are formed in reaction to fear. One woman said that she would never fly in an airplane again after she experienced a very rough flight. She was terrified that the plane was going to crash – a lie. The vow has prohibited her from going on vacations or joining mission trips that were far away.

Vows also involve a form of pride that puts that fence up and basically says, "Step aside, God, I don't trust You to protect me from further pain. I will protect myself." Both of those statements are vows. It is certainly not the conscious intention at the time for most, but that is the consequence. Proverbs 18:10 says, *The name of the* LORD *is a strong tower; the righteous runs into it and is safe.* Choose self-protection or God's protection.

One could make a case for an implied vow that Eve might have made. She knew that she would die if she *ate* the forbidden fruit so she turned God's prohibition into a self-protective vow: I may not or will not *touch* it. And she boldly stated that God told them that they could not eat it or touch it. God never said that they could not touch it. It makes sense that one cannot eat something that they do not touch. It was self-protection. She turned to her own resources rather than to God.

Other vows become problematic if they are reneged. Take the time to ask the Holy Spirit to search your mind for any broken vows. These may include marriage vows, promises, business contracts or agreements, unpaid bills, a pledge to the church building fund, and so on. If one was made and not kept, confess it and make it right if possible. If it seems impossible to fulfill the vow, ask for God's mercy.

Vows can be overt or very subtle. When questioned, some people have said, "Oh, I know exactly what I said!" They are usually the ones who have difficulty renouncing something that they feel justified in holding onto. There are many others who have no idea what the actual or implied vow might have been, so it may take a little prayer time to recognize the vow.

The following verses make clear statements about vows:

*When you make a vow to the LORD your God, you shall not delay to pay it, for it would be sin in you, and the LORD your God will surely require it of you. However, if you refrain from vowing, it would not be sin in you.* Deuteronomy 23:21, 22.

## Sticks and Stones

*When you make a vow to God, do not be late in paying it, for He takes no delight in fools. Pay what you vow! It is better that you should not vow than that you should vow and not pay.* Ecclesiastes 5:4, 5. If you make a vow, keep it. If you think you will not be able to keep a vow, do not make it.

David and Jonathan made vows to each other which extended to future generations. *Then Jonathan made a covenant with David...* 1 Samuel 18:3 Then *Jonathan made David vow again ...* 1 Samuel 20: 17. David said years after the deaths of Saul and Jonathan, *"Is there yet anyone left of the house of Saul, that I may show him kindness for Jonathan's sake?"* 2 Samuel 9:1. David wanted to fulfill the vows that he made to his best friend, Jonathan. He found Jonathan's son, restored his inheritance, and honored him.

*But cursed be the swindler who has a male in his flock, and vows it, but sacrifices a blemished animal to the LORD...* Malachi 1:14. Those who did not fulfill their vows were called swindlers and they were cursed. God takes vows very seriously.

*... yet because of his oaths and because of his dinner guests, he was unwilling to refuse her.* Mark 6:26. King Herod, a pagan unbeliever, reluctantly beheaded John the Baptist because of his vow to grant his daughter whatever she requested.

## Dr. Lynda L. Irons

*The Jews formed a conspiracy and bound themselves under an oath, saying that they would neither eat nor drink until they had killed Paul.* Acts 23:12-14. Even though these men did not kill Paul at that time, they subjected themselves to an oath and the consequence for failure to fulfill that vow. I have often wondered if they were adamant enough to starve themselves to death since they were unable to kill Paul.

As we see from the above examples, vows can be beneficial or they can bring unwanted consequences. They can be obvious or hidden. They can be overt or implied. It would be prudent to ask the Holy Spirit to help you search for any troublesome vows that may need to be addressed. There are sample prayers in chapter ten that can be customized as needed.

# 3
# CURSES

Just what is a curse? Some people think of curses as vulgar strings of expletives, or taking the Lord's name in vain, or speaking some form of evil upon another person. The Greek and Hebrew definitions indicate that curses are far more than any of that. Curses can be quite severe and possibly carry consequences into future generations.

The Greek definitions can mean anything from being trifling or light to wishing or speaking evil out of malevolence. There are other meanings such as non-blessings, belittling, and wishing evil against a person or thing. According to Vine's Complete Expository Dictionary, cursing includes the idea of making someone little or contemptible. An example of that would be to dishonor or belittle one's father or mother. Vine's translates *kakologeo* as "to speak evil" (*kakos*, "evil;" *lego*, "to speak"). Anathema is a

Greek and English word that can mean cursed or a formal curse.

Another aspect of a curse involves the expected consequence upon a person who broke a vow or agreement or covenant. This is why it is important to search for any broken vows. Often the curse was incorporated into the oath or covenant as in the case of Laban and Jacob which was recorded in Genesis 31:44 - 53. They essentially said that if either one of them crossed the line that they had established to do the other one harm, God would judge him with a curse.

And finally, someone who was accursed was said to be in disfavor with God. Judas would be a prime example of one who was accursed because of his betrayal of Jesus. Psalm 109:17, 18 records a prophecy about him. *He also loved cursing, so it came to him and he did not delight in blessing, so it was far from him. But he clothed himself with cursing as with his garments and it entered his body like water, and like oil into his bones.*

Inadvertent curses can be thoughtlessly spoken and/or received. Parents, pastors, teachers, and other authority figures may be motivated by a desire to instruct or warn or admonish. Faulty processing or misinterpretations by children often result in the acceptance of the words which were then processed negatively and essentially became curses. Strongholds form and demonic oppressors take full advantage of the situation. Demons are legalists and they are squatters.

*Like a sparrow in its flitting, like a swallow in its flying, so a curse without cause does not alight.* Proverbs 26:2. Everything that is spoken near, at, over, against, or by you does not necessarily result in a curse. The enemy only has limited so-called legal rights. Among them are:

- He can operate within God's judgment.
- He can operate in an area where God's Word is violated.
- He can operate in a situation in which God has given him permission.
- He can operate if he can deceive you into believing a lie.

A person will be cursed or oppressed or experience consequences because of a curse *with* cause if he finds himself in one of those situations. Francis Frangipane states in The Place of Immunity, "Satan only has the power to manipulate within God's judgment, therefore if there is oppression, it is the result of a curse with cause."

Think of Cain who was cursed by God, and yet, in God's mercy, he was given a mark so that he would not be murdered. Think of the curses pronounced against Adam and Eve, the serpent, and the land.  Think of Job and the devastation that came to his life at the request of Satan and by the permission of God to refine him.  Think of Balaam who tried, but could not curse the Israelites.

In the New Testament, we think of Judas.  *Cursed is every one who hangs on a tree.*  Galatians 3:13.  He committed suicide and hung himself on a tree.  1 Corinthians 5 describes a situation in which the church failed to discipline the immorality of one of its members.  The immoral man was delivered *to Satan for the destruction of his flesh, that his spirit may be saved in the day of the Lord Jesus.*  1 Corinthians 5:5.

A child looks at himself and his world through lenses that can be tainted by word-curses.  The mother who told her child, "Stop crying, you're being weak," was trying to keep her child from being perceived as weak.  The mother wanted to spare her child the same bullying she had endured as a child.  Instead, the enemy twisted her words into something that was used as a curse against the child.  That little girl shut down her emotions with a vow.  She essentially said, "I can't let anyone know I'm weak, therefore, I will never let anyone know that I'm hurt."  She continued to suppress her true feelings even as an adult.

Another child who was bullied got this response from his parents: "You must have asked for it.  It's your fault."  This child grew up taking the blame for everything that went against him because he believed his parents' assessment.  He learned to avoid taking his problems to his parents and locked that response in with an implied vow: "They never believe me, why bother telling them?"  As an untended consequence, it also crippled his relationship with God because he believed the lie that God was like his parents.  Self-curses resulted in a miserable life until they were renounced as an adult.

A middle school boy cruelly taunted a classmate about her body.  She retorted, "Oh yeah, well your face won't be so nice to look at some day!"  Looking back as an adult, she had no idea why she said that.  She was astonished that when she saw him years later, his face was horribly pitted by acne scars.  "Did I curse him by what I said?"  The boy's taunts were sinful.  He was reaping what he had sown and therefore, he experienced the result of a curse *with* cause.

Why do some curses seem to have a significant impact while others seem to do no harm?  Again, the enemy only has the power to operate where there is a stronghold established because of sin.  It is interesting that the young man in the above example was afflicted in his body after cursing the girl's body.  It appears that he reaped what he had sown.

Note also that God pronounced many of the curses that are found in the Bible. They were the result of His just judgments for violations of His laws. Righteousness and justice are the foundations of His throne. The following are more samples from the Old and New Testaments.

Immediately after The Fall, God explained the curses that Adam and Eve and the serpent/Satan sustained in Genesis 3:16, 17. The serpent would be cursed more than all other animals, it would crawl on its belly, eat dust all the days of its life, and there would be enmity between Satan's seed and the woman's seed. Satan would be bruised on his head, but her seed would be bruised on the heel.

The woman was cursed with greatly multiplied pain in bringing forth children. This encompasses more than just labor and delivery; it is the anguish of a mother for the hardships she sees her child experience and more. The woman was also cursed with the desire to rule over her husband, but God said that he shall rule over her. A woman who is constantly in agony about her children – even adult children – is living under the curse. A woman who wants to rule her husband is as well.

The man would experience the cursed ground so that he would have to toil and sweat in order to get a good crop of food. A man who is not providing bread for his family and is not taking dominion is living under the curse.  These curses would extend to all future generations unless there is repentance and intentional renunciations of the curses so that the blessings and goodness of God can be enjoyed.

Numbers 12 gives the account of Aaron and Miriam speaking against their younger brother, Moses.  Miriam was then cursed with leprosy and put out of the camp for a week until she was cleansed and healed.  They had spoken against God's appointed leader and suffered the consequence: she had leprosy for a week, and the entire nation had their journey interrupted for that week as well.

1 Samuel 2:31, 32 and 3:13 tells of another curse.  Because of Eli's knowledge of his sons' sins and neglecting to rebuke them, God said that He would cut off Eli's strength so that there will not be an old man in his house forever.  This curse had an immediate effect in that both sons were killed in a battle, and later, subsequent generations were cut off.  *Solomon dismissed Abiathar from being priest to the LORD, in order to fulfill the word of the LORD, which He had spoken concerning the house of Eli in Shiloh.*  1 Kings 2:27

2 Samuel 21:1-14 describes a three year famine that came to the land during David's reign because Saul, his predecessor, broke the covenant that Joshua made with the Gibeonites prior to his reign.

It cost the lives of seven of Saul's descendants to release the entire nation from the curse. David inherited a curse that came from a previous administration. He became responsible for making it right.

There have been churches and other organizations who suffered consequences because of the decisions of previous administrations. It is vital for churches, organizations, and families to deal with any sins of the previous leaders.

Note: For more in-depth discussion of these issues, please refer to <u>What's in Your Family Tree?</u> by this author.

The following curses were incurred upon the nation of Israel by the leaders of Israel. Just as Aaron, as the high priest, was able to enter the Holy of Holies bearing the names of the tribes on his shoulders – thereby representing their interests and gaining their atonement, so the leaders in subsequent generations could incur negative consequences for the nation. Without going into detail here, I will just state that the leader of a family or a group or an organization has the authority to speak for the whole. That is why it is prudent *not* to be yoked with unbelievers in marriage, business, organizations, political parties, or other alliances.

## Sticks and Stones

After King Solomon died, his son, King Rehoboam alienated ten tribes. Their leaders rebelled. *"What portion do we have in David? We have no inheritance in the son of Jesse; to your tents, O Israel! Now look after your own house, David!" So Israel has been in rebellion against the house of David to this day.* 1 Kings 12:16, 19. There has been historical and present day rebellion against the house of David and his descendant, Jesus. Paul confirmed their hardness of heart. *But by their transgression salvation has come to the Gentiles, to make them jealous. ... a partial hardening has happened to Israel until the fullness of the Gentiles has come in...* Romans 11:11, 25. God preserved a remnant and redeemed the situation and fulfilled the promise to Abraham that through him, the nations would be saved.

The Jewish leaders, speaking for the nation, declared this self-curse regarding the crucifixion of Jesus: *His blood shall be on us and on our children.* Matthew 27:25. Think of the implications of this statement upon future generations. Indeed, much persecution came to the Jews. They were called "Christ killers." That persecution was carried out by the Romans back in that day, by Hitler in more recent times, and by more frequent anti-Israeli sentiments currently.

During a prayer session with a pastor, he revealed that he had some Jewish ancestors. When I spoke Matthew 27:25 aloud, he responded with a grunt and bent over as if he had been punched in the gut. He confessed the sins of his fathers and appealed to God to move his family out from under that curse. He reported a sense of peace and stated that he felt lighter.

Another self-curse by the Jewish leaders occurred when they were given the choice of having Jesus, the Prince of Peace, released to them or Barabbas – a murderer, thief, and insurrectionist. *Away with this man, and release for us Barabbas!* Luke 23:18. They released a curse of insurrection, theft, and murder against their nation. A look at the history of the Jewish people will show the many times that they were subjected to this curse. They have not often lived in peace. They have been murdered, and thieves have taken land and possessions from them as individuals and as a nation.

One more illustration of a curse by these leaders came when they denied their Messiah. *We have no king but Caesar.* John 19:15. Caesar was the Roman ruler. They violated God's warning. *You may not put a foreigner over yourselves.* Deuteronomy 17:15. Caesar and Rome represent the world system: financial, military, legal, religious, and more. The Jews have been living under Roman rule rather than the Theocracy for which they were chosen.

# Sticks and Stones

Principles and Insights Regarding Curses

1. <u>It often affects more than just the one who is cursed</u>. Adam and Eve's choices have affected the whole human race. The descendants of Abraham and Eli and David and so many others who experienced a curse would reap what their forefathers had sown.

A young woman was blasted by her adoptive mother's appraisals. "You're not pretty." "You look like your birth mother." "You're a disappointment." "You were hard to raise." "When you grow up, you slut, your kids will stomp on your heart." It is little wonder that she became promiscuous as a teenager. Later, she was violently gang raped. Her adopted mother's response to the rape was, "Your dancing brought it on; it's your fault." "People who have been raped are second class." She then assessed herself in self-curses, "I'm no good anyway because Mom said I was a whore." "I'm damaged goods, who would want me?" She often wished the rapists would have just killed her. She felt tainted, shameful, guilty, rejected, suicidal, and more. The adoptive mother set many negative things in motion with her curses. Her children reaped many consequences as well.

2. <u>It will often cost others their resources, time, life, etc</u>. Aaron and Miriam's choice and subsequent curse caused the entire nation to have to wait for

her to be healed.  Joshua's hasty covenant and Saul's disregard for that covenant cost the next king and all of the people to suffer from a lengthy famine. Seven of Saul's descendants and their loved ones paid a dear price generations later.  Gehazi's descendants would be afflicted with leprosy because of his greed.

A young man was inundated by his father's criticisms since he was a little boy – "You will never make it." "You're not good enough; nothing you do is good enough." "You make stupid decisions." "You don't handle your money right." "You're not good at structuring yourself."  It is no surprise that his appraisal of himself reflected the things he heard from his father – "I can't do anything right." "I put myself down first so someone else doesn't do it." "I have no self-control." "I foul everything up."  Is it any wonder he suffers from depression?  Or that he has trouble holding a job?  Or that he is reluctant to try new things?  Sadness and hopelessness pervaded his life.  He was filled with anger, shame, and confusion.  There were costly repercussions for him, his wife, and his children.

3. <u>It may impact present and future generations or administrations.</u>  David made a most unwise decision when he took Bathsheba, got her pregnant, and had her husband, Uriah, brought home. When Uriah did not go home to his wife, David had him killed in order to cover up what he had done.

## Sticks and Stones

Perhaps he learned this from his predecessor, King Saul, who sent David to war against the Philistines and hoped that David would have been killed by them.

David's sins brought a curse upon himself and future generations. Not only were there numerous sexual scandals within his immediate family, God imposed another curse. *'You have struck down Uriah the Hittite with the sword, have taken his wife to be your wife, and have killed him with the sword of the sons of Ammon. Now therefore, the sword shall never depart from your house, because you have despised Me and have taken the wife of Uriah the Hittite to be your wife.' Thus says the Lord, 'Behold, I will raise up evil against you from your own household…'* 2 Samuel 12:9 – 11.

A teenager had difficulty falling asleep and staying asleep because of anxious thoughts. As I prayed with him and his parents, the Lord took us to the pregnancy in which the mother was anxious and sleepless because of her high stress job. When this son was born, the doctor declared, "Oh, you will be up with him. You'll never sleep." She experienced just that, and was afraid to have another child because of how difficult those years were.

They prayed and took authority over that curse and prayed blessings over their son. He was able to sleep peacefully from that point on. The family suffered the absence of other children because of the curse. Did the doctor malevolently curse them? No, I do not think so. He made an observation based upon experience. The enemy took advantage of the mother's fear and twisted the words into a curse.

In light of the previous illustrations and principles, it would be prudent to pray that the Holy Spirit would reveal any hidden curses or self-curses that may have tainted your life or the lives of your families. There are sample prayers in chapter ten that can be customized.

# 4
# JUDGMENTS

𝔄 woman was running late and was hurrying to get to work downtown. She was held up in the left turn lane by a parked car. Her frustration mounted with the wasted minutes and she judged the inconsiderate driver to be an idiot. About that time, she noticed that the "idiot" was helping an elderly woman get out of the offending vehicle and into a wheelchair. She immediately confessed her judgments and felt her anger and frustration subside.

"He has two speeds: Slow and stop." A sensitive boy was assailed with words that deeply wounded. Subsequent references to the pace of his daily performances fanned the flames in the tender wounds as they resounded within his soul even as an adult. The observation of his father was effectively a judgment which paralyzed the young man as he embraced his father's opinion. It then became a self-judgment. Was the father an evil man? No, not at all; the enemy preyed upon the youngster.

The woman judged. The boy was judged. In this fallen world, there is an enemy who takes full advantage of any judgment which establishes strongholds. Personality, gender, birth order, age, disposition, history, and other dynamics are factors in a person's response to whatever is vocalized. Who cannot think of something that was spoken over or about them that still reverberates unpleasantly while siblings or classmates were unaffected by the same words in the same or similar situations?

Often the judgment has enough truth within it to be convincing. Circumstances and life events further prove the "truth" of the judgment. The judgment may have come from someone else, likely a parent or significant authority figure, or it may be the result of the way it was processed and interpreted. Self-judgments are just as harmful as judgments from others.

Cindy Jacobs wrote this about bitter root judgments: "The judgments we make in bitterness actually start a cycle that will cause us to fall into the same set of situations over and over until we deal with the root issues in our lives."

## Sticks and Stones

Regardless of the source, it will have a negative effect upon body, soul, spirit, emotions, behavior, and attitudes. Some judgments are very subtle, yet they can have far-reaching effects. Again, it is not simply a matter of denying them, gutting it out, or repeating Scripture verses over and over again or it would have been resolved and the target person would have moved on by now.

All judgments are not bad, however. Sometimes they are merely evaluations to help with a decision. There is no evil intent; there are no troublesome consequences. Numerous judgments must be made every day. Shall I wear the blue one or the green one? Should I take that job or apply for a better one? Should I plant more peppers or grow more tomatoes this year?

The kinds of judgments that are especially problematic are those done with condemnation in mind. Many times it is difficult to separate a curse from a judgment. Indeed, it may be a combination of both. The judgments we address here are not the benign judgments of decision making, rather the malevolent judgments that bring wounds to self and others. We can be the target of a judgment or the hurler of a judgment.

Sometimes we do not realize that we are pronouncing judgments. Perhaps someone points it out and the justification comes: "Well, it's true." or

"Oh, it was a joke; I was just kidding." There may be consequences regardless of how innocent, ignorant, or willful a judgment is. Remember that the enemy is a legalist and a squatter.

One woman judged her mother, embraced a deception, and sealed her attitude with an implied vow. "Because I can't trust my own mother, I can't trust anyone." It may have been wise to distrust her mother, but what she did not realize was that God was inadvertently included in the "anyone" category. She lived a life that bordered on paranoia with no one to whom she could turn.

Looking at the Greek definitions, we find the root words, *krites* (pronounced kree-tays), *krino*, or *krima* where we get our American words such as critical or criminal. One word means to assume the office of a judge, to distinguish, choose, or to give an opinion upon. It can also mean a judgment by a judge to pass a sentence or verdict upon someone. These are objective judgments that should not bring a problem.

God is the judge of all. ... *against all the gods of Egypt I will execute judgments – I am the* LORD. Exodus 12:12. There are numerous verses in the Bible that emphasize the judgeship of God. He is the Judge of all. He is the one and only Lawgiver and Judge. He is the righteous Judge. If someone usurps God's jurisdiction by judging in an area in which there is no authority or responsibility, there will be consequences. God alone understands the motives of the heart.

Other judgments can cause backlash. By illicitly proclaiming a judgment against someone or by pronouncing condemnation, there may be consequences. Judgment can also mean a decision passed on the faults of others. *Do not judge so that you will not be judged. For in the way you judge, you will be judged; and by your standard of measure, it will be measured to you.* Matthew 7:1, 2. Jesus is giving the warning that if you decide to judge others, you are choosing that same judgment for yourself.

It would be beneficial to look at some of the predominant reasons people make negative or presumptuous judgments. Some of the reasons can cause unwanted and unintended consequences and/or awkward situations.

1. <u>Inadequate information.</u> We may not have enough information to make a sound judgment. We often do not see the complete picture, we do not know the whole history, and we do not understand the plans of God. While we try to do the best we can with the facts we have, we do not always have enough details to make an accurate assessment of a person or situation.

A teenager was judged to be promiscuous by her peers. She had gained weight and looked pregnant. After the fifteen pound ovarian cyst was removed, they judged that she had gone for an abortion. She felt humiliated and angry that she was not believed.

A woman was judged to be a snob by her friends because she did not wave back at them. What they did not know was that the woman carefully disguised the fact that she was legally blind. She was unable to see them wave at her from that distance.

A man was judged because he "held his mouth funny." The person who judged him did not know that the man held his mouth that way because his lip was split open by a hockey puck when he was a teenager and the moustache-covered scar caused a slight deformity.

Brothers judged their youngest brother as boastful and arrogant. They did not know that God had a plan for Joseph who would save those very brothers from starvation and poverty.

Eli accused Hannah of drunkenness in 1 Samuel 1:12, 13. He saw her lips moving but did not hear her speaking while she was praying. Perhaps he assumed that she was like his own sons who were known for their drunkenness. He wrongfully judged her.

2. <u>Repetitive behavior or attitudes.</u> When a person or a class of people repeatedly says or does something, others can fairly accurately predict that the person or persons will do it again. They will continue to repeat the habit until there is intervention of some sort.

A woman is judged by her friends and family members to be a gossip because her history bears it out. They would often say, "If you want the world to know, tell Jane."

Another woman judged herself and all men because her husband cheated on her. "If I'm not good enough for a jerk, how can I be good enough for a nice man? Nice guys aren't attracted to me. Something's wrong with me." According to her judgment, all men were either cheaters or not attracted to her. She judged herself to be inferior and defective. Lies and implied vows kept her bound to a lonely life.

"I already know what he's going to say." This teenager had enough experience with his father's answers to his requests that he quit asking for permission and did what he deemed necessary to do what he wanted to do or to get what he wanted to get.

Micaiah, a prophet of God, was judged by King Ahab because *he never prophesies good concerning me but always evil.* 2 Chronicles 18:7. Later when Micaiah gave an unfavorable prophesy about King Ahab, he said, *"Did I not tell you that he would not prophesy good concerning me, but evil?"* 2 Chronicles 18:17. King Ahab would have done well to change his ungodliness to avoid unfavorable prophesies.

3. Prejudice. This word comes from two words: pre and judge. A prejudgment is made and the object of that prejudice is rarely given an impartial opportunity to prove otherwise. It may be a personal prejudgment or something passed down family lines. Roget's Thesaurus says that prejudice is an inclination for or against that which inhibits impartial judgment. Bias.

Many people confess that generations of their family have been prejudiced against an entire class of people. It is often because of the experience of one person. There may have been a single encounter with a certain situation, gender, race, religion, animal, corporation, etc. Everyone and everything else that fits into that category in the same way is subsequently viewed with prejudice.

Prejudice is fear-driven. One or more incidents will cement prejudice into place. How many people are afraid of *all* dogs because they were attacked by *one* particular dog earlier in life? Prejudgments are used as an excuse or rationale in a number of situations. It is why some people no longer attend church. Others do not trust the opposite gender. Still others do not trust anyone in a certain age group.

Many will have an initial hurtful encounter and then, because it involved a sin against them, a stronghold will have been established. The enemy will then draw them into similar scenarios with the same type of people. The inevitable conclusion will then be that this will always happen, or all people in that category are like that. History and experience bears it out and it becomes a self-fulfilling prophecy of sorts.

An incest survivor concluded that all men want only one thing. She judged every man that she ever encountered in the same way. Because of the stronghold that was established early in her life, she did encounter more than one perpetrator and thus, "proved" her beliefs. What she did not know until she received healing and the destruction of the strongholds, was that the demons drew predatory men into her life.

A man would never purchase a Ford. All his life he purchased other vehicle brands. A look at his family history revealed that his father once worked at a Ford plant. When there were lay-offs, his father was among the first to be let go because he did not drive a Ford. That bias – mixed with a little revenge – was passed down to subsequent generations.

Jews were prejudiced against Samaritans and Gentiles. Women were considered to be inferior as well. In John 4 it is recorded that the disciples were surprised that Jesus wanted to pass through Samaria. They were astounded that he would even speak to a Samaritan, and a woman at that!

4. <u>The log and speck syndrome.</u> *Why do you look at the speck that is in your brother's eye, but do not notice the log that is in your own eye? Or how can you say to your brother, 'let me take the speck out of your eye,' and behold, the log is in your own eye? You hypocrite, first take the log out of your own eye, and then you will see clearly to take the speck out of your brother's eye.* Matthew 7:3 – 5.

How many times has someone criticized another person and those around him or her thought, "You should talk!" because he or she obviously had the identical problem? Or worse! It is frequently evident in the other person, but not in the one doing the criticizing. If there is discomfort about an issue in someone else, ask the Lord if it is because of an identical issue in yourself. *If* that is the source of the critical judgment, it may be time to confess and ask the Lord to empower you to make the changes in your own life first.

## Sticks and Stones

A woman tolerated her husband's weight problem until she put on a few extra pounds herself. Then she became critical of his obesity. When she lost weight, his weight did not bother her nearly as much.

"She's just a slut!" A young woman made a declaration about another young woman. She was asked by her friend what her definition of a slut was. "Someone who sleeps around," she replied. The friend then responded, "Excuse me, but isn't that what you have been doing since high school?"

"I hate passive people! They just let life happen to them." A woman angrily criticized and judged her sister's apparent helplessness in a situation. After prayer to get to the root of that kind of anger, she discovered that she was really angry at herself for her own helplessness when she was abused as a child. Her anger was directed at those who reminded her of herself.

The Pharisees criticized the recently healed blind man, but could not see their own spiritual blindness. Jesus replied, *"For judgment I came into this world, so that those who do not see may see, and that those who see may become blind." Those of the Pharisees who were with Him heard these things and said to Him, "We are not blind too, are we?" Jesus said to them, "If you were blind, you would have no sin; but since you say, 'We see;' your sin remains."* John 9:39 – 41.

5. <u>Underlying emotions</u> often drive the judgments against others.  It may come out as criticism or gossip or anger.  These strong negative emotions are frequently directed at self but are expressed about others as we noted in the preceding section.

Fear may be the most prevalent negative emotion.  It may be the primary emotion, but fear also frequently drives other emotions such as anger, hurt, frustration, and rejection.  Negative emotions lead to judgments and subsequently to harmful consequences.

A teenager who lived in a very critical family absorbed the negative messages from siblings and parents and concluded, "I'm bad and unlovable therefore I'll make them reject me."  This teen then went on to prove their judgments were true with additional bad behavior.  It was as if he could control the depth of their rejection by setting himself up for a controlled amount of rejection.

Another man who admitted his fear of rejection said, "It will happen anyway, so I might as well make it happen and get it over with."  He said and did obnoxious things which gave him his expected result.  His judgment of others' response to him spawned vows and locked him into more rejection.

## Sticks and Stones

An obese woman said, "I will be rejected, so I orchestrate it so that it happens on my terms." She hated her own obesity. She judged that others would be prejudiced against her and reject her because of it. Her fear of rejection drove her anger which came out in the form of sarcasm. She rationalized that they judged and rejected her because of the sarcasm rather than the obesity. That was easier to accept. The unspoken fear was that if she lost weight and was still rejected, there was something really wrong with her.

Another said, "My brother is the perfect one; I am never good enough. I have no reason to live." This woman battled suicidal impulses for most of her life. Her belief in the lies led to self-judgments and near fatal consequences.

Saul was angry and afraid of David's rise in popularity and judged that David was trying to gain his throne. *Then Saul became very angry, for this saying displeased him; and he said, "They have ascribed to David ten thousands, but to me they have ascribed thousands. Now what more can he have but the kingdom?" Saul looked at David with suspicion from that day on.* 1 Samuel 18:8, 9. Those were ugly emotions – anger, envy, displeasure, jealousy, fear, suspicion, and probably many more.

6. <u>Personal history</u> can leave anyone with a bias about situations and people. If there are consistent

experiences of stress or trauma, it is natural to make a judgment about that kind of situation. It may come from church experiences or school incidents or medical events or any number of common occasions or encounters.

One person fears all dogs because he was attacked by a dog as a child. Another person still loves dogs and understands that it was just that one mean dog that bit her as a child. Whether it is an animal, a crowd, a church or school incident, judgments are often made that result in long-standing prejudice.

Some people project their own experiences onto everyone else. A young woman who just had rotator cuff surgery came to church in a sling. An older woman inquired about it and commented, "Oh, I had shoulder trouble when I was younger; your shoulder will never be the same." The young woman wisely rebuffed this judgment. With time and therapy, her shoulder became completely healed.

"My grandparents divorced; my parents divorced. It will happen to me, too." This may be an accurate observation of family history, but it does not guarantee that he will be divorced. However, clinging to the judgment will bring unfavorable results. Familial spirits may be a factor here as well.

# Sticks and Stones

Paul wrote a warning to Titus. *One of themselves, a prophet of their own, said, "Cretans are always liars, evil beasts, lazy gluttons."* Titus 1:12. It was a judgment backed up by experience and observations.

7. <u>A spiritual gift.</u> The Holy Spirit may cause discernment or a word of knowledge to manifest for a particular situation. The purpose of this manifestation is for warning or edification so that the discerning believer can pray more effectively about the person or situation. Without understanding the gifts of the Holy Spirit it may have felt like judgment because there was not a tangible shred of evidence to support the thoughts.

A woman went to a tourist attraction that featured an Indian tribe. They were handling snakes and fire. It was a fascinating demonstration, but she became increasingly agitated and had to leave. "It's demonic!" she declared. She felt very judgmental and critical. Years later, after understanding the gifts of the Holy Spirit, she came to realize that she had discerned the spirits of an ancient culture. It was a pagan ritual that drew on power that was not of God.

A man visited his parents' church. During the service three women stood up, interrupted each other as they loudly spoke in tongues. He felt his hair rise up on his neck. He became agitated and thought, "They're blaspheming!" Feeling quite judgmental, he left the service because he did not realize that he was correctly discerning the erroneous use of tongues in that service. While he did not know the interpretation of their words, he sensed that they were speaking blasphemies.

In conclusion, to judge someone else is to usurp God's job and step into an area that is not within one's rightful jurisdiction. This kind of judging is referring to pronouncing judgment rather than an innocuous, objective evaluation. Pride is at the root of this.

Whatever the reason for the judgment by self or others, there is the strong potential for harm. A lie is believed, an event is processed inaccurately, a judgment is made, and a vow entrenches the wounded soul in web of deceit. Strongholds are created and the enemy gleefully takes full advantage of the situation.

The good news is that the wounds can be healed, the strongholds can be demolished with our weapons that are powerful to do so, and demons can be renounced. Once the old is put off, the new can be put on: fruit of the Holy Spirit, favor, and all the goodness that the Lord has stored up for those who fear Him.

# 5
# EFFECTS OF VERBAL ASSAULTS

𝔄ll aspects of a believer's life should reflect the values of the Kingdom of God. This is especially true of thoughts and words. *Finally, brethren, whatever is true, whatever is honorable, whatever is right, whatever is pure, whatever is lovely, whatever is of good repute, if there is any excellence and if anything worthy of praise, let your mind dwell on these things.* Philippians 4:8. Paul was a man who experienced the opposite of those things in so many of his circumstances.

It is important to be familiar with the effects of verbal assaults on both the speaker and the recipient of the lies, vows, curses, and/or judgments. Awareness of these kinds of verbal assaults will bring an appreciation for the principle that to the degree that verbal assaults are allowed or promoted as an accepted part of life, there will be consequences and repercussions. Lack of awareness of spiritual principles does not grant a free pass.

Again, there is sin involved with verbal assaults. That sin creates a stronghold. Demons use the stronghold as a platform from which to oppress. Demons can then draw the oppressed one into similar situations with the same type of destructive people. Verbal assaults cause emotional pain. Emotional pain often causes the generation of more verbal assaults. It is vitally important to recognize and address the ramifications of having verbal assaults sown, cultivated, and reaped.

Jesus loved to demonstrate fundamental spiritual teachings by using illustrations from natural law. Natural principles have parallel spiritual principles. One such natural law is the law of sowing and reaping. Understanding natural laws gives insight into the principles of the higher spiritual laws. These are reassuring principles if we are sowing not just heroic gestures, but also the myriad of ordinary courtesies of daily living and thus, reap reward in time as well as eternity.

- You reap what you sow.
- You reap later than you sow.
- You reap more than you sow.
- You reap only if you sow.
- You reap where you sow.

# Sticks and Stones

Pumpkin seeds produce pumpkin plants which produce several pumpkins. Each pumpkin has many seeds within it which are capable of producing a huge field of pumpkin plants, and that generation of pumpkins is capable of producing yet another generation, and so on. There cannot be expectations of a crop of pumpkins if pumpkin seeds were not planted. One will look for the pumpkins where they were planted, that is, in the pumpkin patch.

In the spiritual realm, the same principles apply. We will reap *what* we sow – curses or blessings, generosity or stinginess, favor or prejudice, trouble or peace, deep relationships or shallow friendships, or any other tangible or intangible item. Thoughtfulness about the potential positive or negative effects of the things that are sown is imperative.

There was a season in which I was not receiving many donations for my counseling work. I asked the Lord if I could tithe my time, that is, use an arbitrary figure of thirty dollars per hour and when I was not paid for my work, then it would be as if I had tithed thirty or sixty or ninety dollars that week. After several weeks, I realized that I had an abundance of free time on my hands. The Lord taught me that if I wanted to reap dollars, I needed to sow dollars, not time.

You will reap *later* than you sow, that is, in a different season; or perhaps a different generation. You may be reaping something that a previous generation sowed. It may be reaped within a matter of days or decades or centuries. Sometimes it is difficult to determine if something is the result of sowing and reaping or if it is the result of generation after generation accepting attitudes and behaviors that have been modeled by the previous ones.

A quick look at the first seven generations recorded in Genesis gives insight into the above principle. Cain's line produced another murderer, Lamech, by the seventh generation. Seth's line produced righteous men. The question must be asked: Was it nature or nurture, or both? In either case, the reaping of the good or bad occurred in later generations.

You will reap *more* than you sow and the more you sow, the more you will reap – thirty, sixty, or a hundredfold. If you are generous with time and money and other resources, you will receive back more than you gave. It may not come immediately. Children or grandchildren may benefit from things that have been sown.

The following verses say it well. *The generous man will be prosperous, and he who waters will himself be watered.* Proverbs 11:25. *Now this I say, he who sows sparingly shall also reap sparingly; and he who sows bountifully shall also reap bountifully. Now He who supplies seed to the sower and bread for food, will supply and multiply your seed for sowing and increase the harvest of your righteousness.* 2 Corinthians 9:6, 10.

You will reap *if* you sow. There are some who are like the one-talent man who bury their treasure. No one benefits from that tactic. Not the man, not the master, not his family. If you sow positive seeds, then you will benefit, your family will benefit, your church and your community will benefit. And God will get the glory.

Acts 9:36 gives the account of a woman named Tabitha. *This woman was abounding with deeds of kindness and charity, which she continually did.* When she died, those who benefited from her deeds summoned Peter. They displayed all the tunics and garments she had made for them. Peter prayed and she was raised from the dead.

You will reap *where* you sow. You have been given a jurisdiction that is unique to you so that you can bloom where you are planted. Using the plant analogy, once there is maturity, then you can produce fruit which carries the seed. You will sow into the next generation and the one after that for your children and grandchildren.

God knows the motives of the heart; He understands why people sow what they sow. He gives clear warnings about the consequences of disregarding spiritual laws as well as the rewards of observing them. The following are just a few of the Scriptures that illustrate the sowing and reaping principles. Some of them promise great hope. Others contain dire warnings about the effects of verbal assaults and other negative items.

*And Adoni-bezek fled; and they pursued him and caught him and cut off his thumbs and big toes. And Adoni-bezek said, "Seventy kings with their thumbs and their big toes cut off used to gather up scraps under my table; as I have done, so God has repaid me."* Joshua 1:6, 7.

*According to what I have seen, those who plow iniquity and those who sow trouble harvest it.* Job 4:8.

*Those who sow in tears shall reap with joyful shouting. He who goes to and fro weeping, carrying his bag of seed, shall indeed come again with a shout of joy, bringing his sheaves with him.* Psalm 126:5, 6.

*The generous man will be prosperous, and he who waters will himself be watered.* Proverbs 11:25.

*A man will be satisfied with good by the fruit of his words, and the deeds of a man's hands will return to him.* Proverbs 12:14.

## Sticks and Stones

*From the fruit of a man's mouth he enjoys good, but the desire of the treacherous is violence. The one who guards his mouth preserves his life; the one who opens wide his lips comes to ruin.* Proverbs 13:2, 3.

*He who sows iniquity will reap vanity ...* Proverbs 22:8.

*For they sow the wind and they reap the whirlwind.* Hosea 8:7.

*Sow with a view to righteousness, reap in accordance with kindness; break up your fallow ground. You have plowed wickedness, you have reaped injustice, you have eaten the fruit of lies.* Hosea 10:12-13.

*Already he who reaps is receiving wages and is gathering fruit for life eternal; so that he who sows and he who reaps may rejoice together.* John 4:36.

*So then neither the one who plants nor the one who waters is anything, but God who causes the growth. Now he who plants and he who waters are one; but each will receive his own reward according to his own labor.* 1 Corinthians 3:7, 8.

*Now this I say, he who sows sparingly will also reap sparingly, and he who sows bountifully will also reap bountifully.* 2 Corinthians 9:6.

*Now He who supplies seed to the sower and bread for food will supply and multiply your seed for sowing and increase the harvest of your righteousness; you will be enriched in everything for all liberality, which through us is producing thanksgiving to God.* 2 Corinthians 9:10, 11.

*Do not be deceived, God is not mocked; for whatever a man sows, this he will also reap. For the one who sows to his own flesh will from the flesh reap corruption, but the one who sows to the Spirit will from the spirit reap eternal life. Let us not lose heart in doing good, for in due time we will reap if we do not grow weary.* Galatians 6: 7-9.

*And the seed whose fruit is righteousness is sown in peace by those who make peace.* James 3:18.

It is evident that the principles of the law of sowing and reaping also apply to verbal assaults. Three focal issues to consider in evaluating the effects of lies, vows, curses, and/or judgments are (1) the sin of the verbal assault, (2) the stronghold that is established by the sin, and (3) the accompanying demonic oppressors that occupy the stronghold and torment the recipient or producer of the verbal assault. Emotional pain and additional verbal assaults will be addressed in chapter eight.

Because there are so many pastors and believers who have not been taught about these principles, it is worth emphasizing their relevance. There is not one person that I have counseled in twenty-five years who did not need to face these issues which were key to their freedom.

Be aware that any verbal assault may consist of a combination of a lie, a vow, a curse, and/or a judgment. Address each aspect that emerges. The Holy Spirit can then be asked to heal and seal each broken place, and fill with the goodness of God's kingdom. We must put off the old and put on the new.

Let us address the first of these three effects: (1) <u>the sin of pronouncing a verbal assault</u>. This sin may be spoken by a person intentionally or inadvertently to target self or others. To embrace a lie is to be aligned with Satan who is the chief liar and deceiver. To make a vow is to be self-protective rather than to turn to God for protection. To curse or judge self or others is to usurp God's jurisdiction. These are all sins and forms of pride.

Most of us have regretted something that we have said. This is a universal issue. A look through the Bible will reveal quite a number of verbal assaults. Sometimes the words that are spoken, especially in the heat of the moment, are not recognized as a verbal assault. If not recognized and dealt with effectively, the stronghold and oppression will remain.

Jesus said some strong words about judging or cursing someone. *But I say to you that everyone who is angry with his brother shall be guilty before the court; and whoever says to his brother, "You good-for-nothing," shall be guilty before the supreme court; and whoever says, "You fool," shall be guilty enough to go into the fiery hell.* Matthew 5:22.

It is imperative to approach others out of compassion rather than just knowledge. *"Knowledge makes arrogant, but love edifies."* 1 Corinthians 8:1. As a wise friend often says, "Truth without love is brutality. Love without truth is hypocrisy."

The second effect of verbal assaults that must be addressed is (2) the stronghold. Strongholds which are created by the lie, vow, curse, and/or judgment are often ignored. Most of us have been taught that confession and repentance takes care of everything. Sometimes it does, but more often, we must contend with sin and its fruit more thoroughly.

The word translated stronghold or fortress comes from the Greek word *topos* and is the root of our American word topography. It was a military term that described a strategic place from which the enemy could get a good shot at his target. We are told in 2 Corinthians 10:4 that we have weapons that are powerful to demolish strongholds, but if we do not realize that the strongholds even exist, we may keep giving the enemy a platform from which to oppress. And he is probably laughing because we built it for him!

The third aspect of the effects of verbal assaults that must be addressed concerns (3) <u>demonic oppressors</u>. There are many believers who dismiss demonic activity because of the work of Jesus on the cross. An argument could be made for that stance based on Colossians 2:15. *When He had disarmed the rulers and authorities, He made a public display of them, having triumphed over them through Him.* Yes, the enemy has been disarmed; he has lost the battle, but he still has the power to deceive, thwart, lie, and be a thorn in the flesh.

Demons are given a so-called legal right to oppress because of the sin. They dwell in the strongholds that are established by the sin. God would not have included information about our weapons if they were irrelevant. Believers have authority to cast demons out, but may not do so if there is no recognition of their presence or the legal right for them to be there.

Demons feed on sin and dwell in the strongholds that are established by the sin. Is there a demon under every bush? Probably not. However, if there is lack of victory in an area that has been confessed, repented of, and renounced, then dealing with strongholds and demons is often what has been overlooked.

*For though we walk in the flesh, we do not war according to the flesh, for the weapons of our warfare are not of the flesh, but divinely powerful for the destruction of fortresses.* 2 Corinthians 10:3, 4. We are fighting a spiritual battle. We must demolish strongholds and address demonic oppressors with our spiritual weapons.

Peter makes an interesting statement about arming ourselves with the same purpose that Christ had. *Therefore, since Christ has suffered in the flesh, arm yourselves also with the same purpose, because he who has suffered in the flesh has ceased from sin, so as to live the rest of the time in the flesh no longer for the lusts of men, but for the will of God.* 1 Peter 4:1, 2. Our purpose is not to defeat Satan. Christ has done that. Our purpose is to gain a victory over personal sins, personal faults.

Peter is not saying that suffering causes sinless perfection. He is saying that after you have suffered from your fault, as in the case receiving and/or delivering verbal assaults, and have been freed from that fault, you will be able to live for God's will, not self-will. A repentant judgmental person, for example, can more readily discern a critical spirit, knows what to do about it, and is equipped to compassionately minister to others with the same issue.

# 6
# LISTENING FOR VERBAL ASSAULTS

This is where the rubber meets the road. Since lies, vows, curses, and judgments are verbal in nature, it is vital to begin to be trained to recognize them for what they are. If what is said or thought is not identified as a verbal assault, the strongholds and demons associated with them cannot be contended with properly. *For the ear tests words, as the palate tastes food.* Job 34:3.

Dr. James Dobson wrote about this issue in his March, 2004 newsletter. "It concerns the sheer power of words. They are so easy to utter, often tumbling out without much reason or forethought. Those who hurl criticism or hostility at others may not even mean or believe what they have said. Their comments may reflect momentary jealousy, resentment, depression, fatigue or revenge. Regardless of the intent, harsh words sting like killer bees. Almost all of us, including you and me, have lived through moments when a parent, a teacher, a friend, a colleague, a husband or a wife said something that cut to the quick. That hurt is now sealed forever in the memory bank. That is an amazing property of the spoken word. Even though a person forgets most of his or her day-by-day experiences, a particularly painful comment may be remembered for decades. By contrast, the individual who did the damage may have no memory of the encounter a few days later."

It is important to remember that identical words may be spoken to several people and there will be different responses. For example, a father berates his children. Some of them are greatly impacted by his words while their other siblings are not. Different genders, different personalities, different ages, different experiences, different birth order, and other factors are considerations when it comes to verbal assaults.

The Holy Spirit will speak to our spirits if He has not been quenched. Our redeemed and sanctified mind can discern truth from deceptions. When words assail, there are three principal sources for those verbal assaults:

Self: things thought and believed because of misinterpretation and/or faulty processing.
Others: things spoken over, to, or at us.

Demons: promote deceptions and can influence thinking.

There are several categories of speech which can give an indication that there may be subtle or overt, implied or direct verbal assaults being spoken. There will be examples given in each category. If you recognize a familiar thought, take note of it. There are instructions and prayers in later chapters to help you dismantle their effects in your life.

Practice listening to your own thoughts and verbalizations first. Pay attention to the conversations of others. However, unless there is a loving relationship with someone who is expressing a lie, vow, curse, and/or judgment; it is prudent to remain quiet.

The following examples are actual quotes that have been gathered over several decades. I have italicized the *absolute words* and (bracketed) some *implied* words in each of the categories. Accompanying emotions are not always listed, but it can be easily surmised what they might be.

<u>Absolute words</u>
This is probably the most common category of verbal assaults. These words are all-inclusive. Most of the time, the person who speaks one of these words actually intends for it to be limited to a narrow range of people or situations. However, by

using one of these extreme words, the thought is entrenched and limits are removed. It gives the legalistic demons an opportunity to take advantage by twisting the intention and/or taking it off the charts.

As conversations are listened to, pay attention to your own thoughts. Notice how often the verbal assault contains one or more of the following words. There is an element or a degree of truth that can be found, but use of these words and others like them will consistently be clues to a verbal assault.

*Always – All – Anyone – Anything – Any time – Each*
*Ever – Never – Whenever – Only*
*Everyone – Everything – Every time – Everywhere*
*Nobody – Nothing – None – Nowhere – Anywhere*
*Must – Have to – Cannot – Should/should not – will/will not*

"*Every time* I go to a family gathering, *someone* criticizes me." This may be true, but when questioned, he admitted that he has attended gatherings in which there was no criticism. He goes to gatherings with an attitude that will invite further criticism in the natural. He will have to contend with previously established strongholds as well. *For what I fear comes upon me, and what I dread befalls me.* Job 3:25.

"I've *always* been made fun of by *everyone*." This person is typical of some who can look back at a lifetime of insults. A stronghold was established in her at an early age because of the family atmosphere. There was likely a critical spirit running rampant in that family.

"I just *can't* (ever) please my father." This teen made this observation after several failed attempts to please his demanding father. He made this blanket statement and embraced an implied vow to the effect that he would no longer bother to try to please his father. Needless to say, their relationship was stormy.

"*Nobody* can help me, there's something *very* wrong with me." Helplessness and hopelessness pervaded her life. She was not physically impaired or mentally ill. After consenting to prayer ministry, she discovered that she had buried memories of having been sexually violated at a young age. Messages of the perpetrator were embedded in her mind. Faulty processing further locked her into despair.

"I'm (always) stuck. I *can't* change that. I *always* choose the wrong thing." A few poor choices convinced this young man that he was doomed to be stuck with making wrong decisions. This went back to his father's response to one thoughtless act that is typical of a child. The father did not intend to speak curses and judgments, but once the boy embraced that authoritarian opinion, the enemy took advantage of him.

"I have *no* purpose. I am *always* dissatisfied." This is the conclusion of someone who saw the same attitude demonstrated in her parents. There was much pressure to perform, to excel, to make the family proud. The parents were seldom satisfied with the report cards, athletic ability, and other endeavors.

"*Nobody's* (ever) going to tell me what to do. *Nobody's* (ever) going to get me." Trust was violated. Rebellion was the self-protective response of this wounded young man. These vows resulted in rebellion toward all authority figures. They also locked him out of trusting within any relationship, including one with God.

"I *can't* (ever) have an opinion. I *can't* (ever) express anger." Family rules kept this young woman muted and frustrated. These are deceptions that carry implied vows. Her anger came out in passive-aggressive ways and in various diseases of the digestive tract.

"I *must* keep Mom happy and dance. If I stop, I *will* let my *whole* family down." The child was pressured by the encouragement of her mother, "We're depending on you to make us proud." Her sibling had dropped out of dance and now it was up to her. The mother thought she was giving positive support, but the child misinterpreted the intent.

Verbal Assault Combinations
As previously mentioned, each type of verbal assault will have to be addressed by confession, repentance, renunciation, forgiveness, or other appropriate responses. If only one aspect is detected, there may be continued lack of freedom because of the persistent presence of the verbal assaults that were not yet addressed.

"I (will) hold onto (all) things from the past because if I let go, I *won't* have *anything*." It is a lie that she will have nothing. There is an overt vow that says that she must hold onto all things from the past. This judgment about the effects of letting go has become a self-curse. She lives with fear, distrust, and insecurity. Her vow also keeps her from relying upon God to supply her needs.

"Don't (ever) make me a promise; you'll (always) lie and I'll (always) get angry." This is a lie based on processing past events with failed promises from significant people. She is judging others by presuming that they will also lie to her. She has an implied, if not actual, vow to respond in anger. She not only says "you'll lie," she implies that you will always lie.

"I'll *never* let *anyone* close. I'll make it *impossible* for *anyone* to know the real me." This betrayed and deeply wounded lady has made blatant vows with these statements. The implied vow locks her into presenting a false front. She also prejudged everyone she encountered so she sabotaged relationships. She was frustrated with her inability to grow in her relationship with God, but she unknowingly excluded God from getting close to her as well.

"If you *can't* do it (anything) right the first time, *don't* (ever) bother." This was spoken over this young man by his father who was a perfectionist. He observed that his father appeared to perform tasks well the first time his father attempted it. He judged himself as being inferior because he could not do so. He had a tremendous reluctance to try new things because he unwittingly vowed not to try new things to protect himself from failure and humiliation.

Finding implied verbal assaults
This "formula" helps uncover the implied verbal assault which is most often a vow. It can also clarify the original verbal assault which is usually a lie or deception. Unfortunately, many Christians can also read the Scriptures and have negative emotions because of erroneous applications as is evident from some of the examples.

When there is a sense that something is a verbal assault, but it is not entirely clear or there is uncertainty about what to do with it, it can help to use the following formula. This can also help bring up the implications without making an assumption and without putting words into someone's mouth.

State what has been said, add "therefore" and then record the conclusion. That conclusion will clarify the underlying implications and may uncover another verbal assault. Most often, a vow or an implied vow will be found.

FORMULA:
*State the verbal assault*, add THEREFORE, and <u>fill in the blank</u>

"*No one ever* protects me," THEREFORE, <u>I *must* protect myself</u>. It was obvious that the initial statement brought pain, but what was not stated was actually the source of the person's problem. In this case, it is a vow. The initial lie led to the implied vow which is yet another verbal assault. By embracing the vow, she excluded protection from God and others, and became consumed with self-protection. By embracing the vow, no one could protect her because she must protect herself. There was also a subtle judgment regarding others, including God, being unwilling or unable to protect her. This lady initially came about a present-day situation in which she felt unprotected. After prayer, the Lord reminded her of the rest of the memory in which a pastor entered the room and the threat from another man was eliminated. The truth is that God *did* send someone to protect her. The truth is that she has the ability to be assertive. She experienced peace and her trust in God was restored.

I *can't* (ever) be caught off guard, THEREFORE, I *must* second-guess and analyze everything. A significant event early in this young man's life caused the original lie/vow/self-curse/judgment. His conclusion is another deception and a vow that left him with obsessive-compulsive behavior and many fears that paralyzed him.

"With one vice (always) comes another," THEREFORE, if I have one vice, I *will* eventually get another vice. It's *inevitable.* This person locked himself into cycling through vice after vice – drinking, gambling, smoking, and promiscuity. These lies may also have been his justification for indulging in vices. The implications are self-curses and self-judgments. Another implied vow was that he must always have a vice. Justification and some hopelessness marked his life. He repented and renounced the blatant and implied verbal assaults and was released from all vices.

## Dr. Lynda L. Irons

A teen made a fantastic baseball play, but his father/coach said, "Even a squirrel will get lucky and find a nut once in a while." THEREFORE, <u>why try again?</u> This young man was afraid to try to achieve success a second time once he "got his nut." It extended from the ball field to academics to relationships.

*...no good thing does He withhold from those who walk uprightly.* Psalm 84:11. THEREFORE, <u>since I haven't received much good lately, I must not be upright</u>. A Christian used this verse to explain why he was feeling as if God had turned His back on him.

*The righteous cry and the Lord hears, and delivers them out of all their troubles.* Psalm 34:17. THEREFORE, <u>I must not be righteous because I cry out and I still have troubles</u>. This was another "proof text" for a despondent believer that God does not hear her desperate cries.

*And we know that God causes all things to work together for good to those who love God, to those who are called according to His purpose.* Romans 8:28. Another dejected believer concluded that he must not be called because things were not working out very well.

# Sticks and Stones

<u>Habitual thoughts or statements</u>
Many people can say, "Pick a memory, *any* memory," or "Same song, different verse," or "This *always* happens to me." They describe a history in which there was repetition of the same kinds of circumstances, similar treatment by others, and variations on a very familiar theme. Very often there will be a stronghold that was established earlier in the person's life. Ask the Holy Spirit to reveal the root. It may also come from generational issues which we will not deal with here.

Do not be surprised if the source goes back to the womb experience, especially if the following is said: "I can *always* remember this kind of thing happening." "I have *always* been an angry person." "I've *always* thought that about myself."

An elderly woman came for prayer. She was wearing a cervical collar because of a recent mishap. She stated that she *always* seemed to have issues with her neck. We decided to ask the Holy Spirit to take us to the root of this repeated problem. After a few moments of waiting, she said that she remembered that her mother told her about the circumstances of her birth. It was a home birth and the midwife failed to catch her. She was dropped onto her head and injured her neck. She then began to recount numerous injuries and accidents from childhood until the present in which she was hit on the head and strained her neck. We prayed over these events, pled the blood of Jesus over the stronghold that was established at birth, rebuked tormenting spirits, and asked the Lord to heal and protect and bless her. As of this writing, years later, she has not had another injury of that kind.

Another person was raised in a family that had high expectations. "I *always have to* have the answers. It is *never* acceptable to fail." She was expected to uphold the honor of the family name, to have the best grades, impeccable manners, and the solution to any problem that she encountered. She developed ulcers. She lived with fear, guilt, and shame in spite of putting on a good front for the world.

"I'm (always) just an accident waiting to happen. My parents thought I'd kill myself before age twelve." This rowdy young man was reckless in his boyhood adventures. He had many accidents. His ADHD exacerbated the problem as he did not foresee possible dangers. His declarations were repetitions of his parents' statements. Essentially they were judgments that became self-curses and self-judgments.

"This is just the way I have *always* been. This is just the way I am." This person is like so many others who have expressed this lie and self-judgment. She expressed a fatalistic acceptance of the way she always has been and always will be.

# Sticks and Stones

Some people use it as a justification to remain unchanged. Some succumb to depression and a sense of doom. She accepted the challenge to have Jesus Christ speak to those lies and she received release.

<u>Inherited verbal assaults</u>
These are statements that have been spoken most often by parents and significant authority figures which are then embraced and repeated. Sometimes it is not spoken, rather it is the interpretation based on body language or circumstances. There will be more about this in the Family Rules section below.

"My *whole* family has a bad temper." Whether it was modeled or spoken, this individual used this expression to explain and excuse anger. The expression is a lie/vow/curse/judgment. There were some who did not have a bad temper. The implied vow was, "Since I am a part of this family, I have a bad temper and there is *nothing* I can do about it."

"Dad *always* said, 'You can get screwed once, but *don't* (ever) get screwed twice.'" The father's judgment, based on his own experience, was that you *will* get screwed. This is followed by the implied vows that you *must not* let it happen again and that you *must* protect yourself. Also, by implication there is an element of shame on the son if he should ever get screwed the second time. He would be judged by himself and his father because of it.

"Mom said that *all* men *only* want sex." This is a lie and judgment coupled with an implied vow. Not only will she have to renounce the verbal assaults, she will have to deal with the events in her life that flowed out of them. She embraced negative, judgmental thoughts about men and developed poor relationships with them because she believed that she ought to comply with their demands because she could not fight the inevitable.

We are reminded of Paul's statement to Titus. *One of themselves, a prophet of their own, said, "Cretans are always liars, evil beasts, lazy gluttons."* Titus 1:12. What would it have been like to grow up in Crete with this prophecy echoing in the background?

<u>Conditional Clauses</u>
"If – Then" and "Either – Or" statements are predetermined responses to real or imagined or anticipated events. The conditional clause generally includes a statement and a resultant vow. Also look for deceptions, curses, and judgments. Most of these conditional clauses or ultimatums are delivered primarily with the emotion of anger. Many times fear drives the anger.

*If we let Him go on like this, all men will believe in Him, and the Romans will come and take away both our*

# Sticks and Stones

*place and our nation.* John 11:48. The Pharisees were driven by fear. They believed the deception that they were responsible for keeping the Romans placated. They were also content with the status quo. These beliefs caused them to vow to do away with Jesus.

"If I trust, I *won't* be in control; if I'm not in control, I'll *have to* feel. *I'll* (always) be hurt." This series of deceptions is followed by the implied vows that she *must not* trust, she *must* be in control, she *must* not allow herself to feel. She *will* do what it takes to avoid getting hurt again. Suspicion and fear rule her life. She controls as much as she can because of the lack of control she had as a child when she was violated by someone she should have been able to trust. By renouncing the vows, she was able to begin to trust the Lord to be her defense.

"If he says that to me one more time, I'm going to_____." Variations on this universal declaration are made by so many people. Their vow locks them into fulfilling their threat. They will retaliate in some way. This often involves an act of sin which will further complicate things for them in the spiritual realm with more strongholds and more demonic oppressors.

"If it's my fault, I can fix it." This woman did the mental gymnastics that were necessary to make herself believe that everything that went wrong in her marriage was her fault. If she was not a good enough wife, she could become good enough to salvage the marriage by making adjustments in attitude or behavior that would give her the illusion of being in control of a situation for which she was not responsible. After prayer, she realized the truth – "I have sinned against myself for assuming responsibility." She was set free.

"If I screw up, I (will) get discouraged and quit." This conditional statement drives many painful emotions – fear, depression, shame, and guilt to name a few. There is also reluctance to try new things, or even to try much at all because of the assumption that he will screw up. This person tries to live a safe lifestyle. The problem is the conflict between the desire for a full, rich life and the reluctance to move beyond mediocrity.

"It's my way or the highway." This man's ultimatum has sabotaged many personal and business relationships. Fear was the predominant emotion that drove his anger and alienated those around him.

<u>Statements that have more emotion than a given situation warrants</u>
If a current situation logically calls for an emotional intensity of about a 2 or 3 on a scale of 0 – 10, and a 9 or 10 level of intensity is expressed, ask the Holy Spirit to reveal a previous event that is being

triggered. "Lord, where is *this* kind of anger coming from?" The unresolved emotions from previous events are triggered and dumped on top of the normal level of emotion. There will often be a verbal assault of some kind that will need to be addressed as well.

There are times when a person will respond with "My anger's a 20 on a scale of 0 – 10." That consistently indicates that the natural human anger is exacerbated by demonic oppressors. Look for unforgiveness issues. There is more on this topic in this author's book, Anger at God, Self, and Others.

"Can't you *ever* put *anything* back!?! I can *never* find *anything* when I need it!" There is a judgment and lie that the person *cannot* return things to their proper place. There is a lie about *never* finding *anything*. There is too much emotion for a single misplaced item. Anger and frustration are most apparent, but fear drives these emotions. A look into the person's history revealed that there was an expectation that her spouse would also embrace the "rules" of her family of origin that "there's a place for everything and everything *must* be in its place" and that he understood that there would be trouble for misplaced items. This drove her perfectionism – another fear-driven behavior. She was also feeling disregarded and disrespected because of the repetition of little annoyances like this. Once the Lord brought this connection to her attention, she repented of her anger and released her spouse from the expectations. There was increased peace in the relationship.

"I just want to kill someone today!" The over-the-top level of anger expressed by this teenager was far too intense for his experience at school. He was sent to detention and the other students "looked ugly" at him. The root of this fear-driven anger went back to a childhood memory in which he witnessed a murder. Someone "looked ugly" at his brother's friend so the friend shot the man. After processing this memory, he reported that the original event was peaceful and the anger in the present day situation was down to a 2 on the scale of 0 – 10.

*When Haman saw that Mordecai neither bowed down nor paid homage to him, Haman was filled with rage.* Esther 3:5. Haman sought to destroy, not only Mordecai, but the entire Jewish population. His pride elevated the intensity of his emotions. He vowed to destroy Mordecai. Perhaps he was insecure in that dog-eat-dog society.

<u>Illogic, Faulty Processing, and Misinterpretations</u>
These statements seem to make perfect sense to the one who has embraced them, but they can sound ludicrous to others who hear them. The thoughts are usually the result of some very flawed processing of an actual early life event. The

consequences of these verbal assaults are often quite serious. After the Lord brings His truth, it will be apparent how illogical the thoughts were.

The enemy will often dupe us into believing that there is one and only one solution to a given situation. There is only door A or door B. Sometimes there is a double-bind in which it seems to be a lose – lose situation with no other way out. The beauty of healing is that Jesus can bring a creative, winning solution to counter the duplicity of the enemy. *No temptation* (trial) *has overtaken you but such as is common to man; and God is faithful, who will not allow you to be tempted beyond what you are able, but with the temptation* (trial) *will provide the way of escape also, that you may be able to endure it.* 1 Corinthians 10:13.

"My mother gave me up so I *have to* give up my baby." This adopted woman may also have been driven by generational curses or familial spirits. She aborted her first child because of this verbal assault. She was appalled that she could have, not only believed that lie, but acted on it after she received healing.

"I'm (only) lovable if I'm pretty. I *can't* (ever) be pretty unless I'm sexual. I *can't* (ever) be sexual with God, therefore, He *can't* think I'm pretty." What?! This also came from an early sexual abuse incident of a little girl who was left to process the trauma alone. She continued to believe this imbedded conclusion even as an adult. Her poor relationship with God was compounded by the confusion of the image of her earthly father with that of her Heavenly Father.

"I *can't* love kids like 'normal' people do. I will *never* be a good mom. I'm a *terrible* mother. The devil *will* use me to hurt my kids. I used faulty discipline. I thought I was doing *everything* as a Christian mom; I've (completely) *destroyed* their lives." This well-meaning Christian mother took full responsibility for the outcome of her children's lives. They had problems, but were certainly not destroyed. She lived with so much fear that she bordered on paranoia.

"The *only* thing I could trust was the lie. I *can't* trust God because He is Truth." This man believed that *everyone* lied about *everything*. By embracing that notion, his conclusion about God was logical, yet untrue.

"The Holy Ghost people told me that I did not have enough faith, so get in the car and drive." The legally blind woman did just that. She did not receive her sight and crashed the car.

<u>Transposing a question into a statement</u>
This will clarify and strengthen the verbal assault. Essentially, the person is saying *this* by asking *that*

question. We do not want to put words into someone's mouth, but it is helpful to "challenge" the statements and then find out what drives them. Christians are especially reluctant to express a strong statement that sounds unspiritual, so it gets couched in a question. Putting it into question form takes the edge off, but the strong emotions are still driving the verbal assaults.

"Are there *no* miracles for me?" By transposing the question, it might be stated, "There are *no* miracles for me." This is both a lie and a judgment against God. This young woman had just had a second miscarriage. She was greatly disappointed that her prayers for a baby apparently went unheeded.

"Why does *everything always have to* be so hard?" The statement would be, "*Everything always has to* be so hard." A woman looked at her life and observed that there was not much that was easy or that flowed well. There were a*lways* complications. She was weary and bordered on bitterness toward God.

"*No matter* how hard you try, *nothing* works out. I *always* ask, 'How is this *going to* come back and bite me?'" The question would be stated, "This *is going to* come back and bite me." Another hassled and harried man eyed circumstances with wariness. He was convinced that it *would* come back and bite him.

Several self-protective vows flowed out of these beliefs. He had very little joy.

"Are you stupid?! What in the world is wrong with you!?" The questions would be transposed to state, "You are stupid! There is something wrong with you!" Outrage at a simple mistake brought these strong curses and judgments spewing out of a very frustrated parent. The parent had old messages and old fears triggered that were projected onto the child. The child reacted with vows to the effect that he *will not* attempt *anything* difficult. There is much shame and guilt and other emotions to process when the parent does not try to mitigate the damage.

## Clichés and Old Sayings

Clichés, proverbs, adages, maxims, mottoes, and other old sayings have longevity because they contain some proven wisdom. They are common sense observations and may be quite appropriate for a given situation, however, watch for subtle verbal assaults. Note in the first part of the list below, there are several pairs of opposites. Which one is right?

Most of the time, speaking these things is no big deal. However, there is potential for trouble when one of these sayings is embraced, twisted in some way, or taken to an extreme. For example, the child who is told that idle hands are the devil's workshop may be compelled to stay busy all the time. He will feel fearful or guilty for being idle. He may feel as if he is evil when he is not doing something at all times. His sibling may be completely unaffected by hearing this.

A grade school girl ran into a classmate as they rushed to the piano. The teacher fixed her stern eyes on her and said, "Haste makes waste!" The girl felt condemnation, shrank back into the group, but thought, "No, it doesn't." She made an implied vow to prove that it did not. She was driven by the vow to hurry, to be efficient, to be economical, and more from then on. Those things are not necessarily bad, but she always felt that drive until she was released through prayer. She also realized another truth: the teacher also looked sternly at the other child.

Rather than making a comment on each of the items, let me challenge you to imagine that the person to whom one of these was spoken has unhealed issues. Then think about what kind(s) of verbal assault(s) are either obvious or implied. Next, think about the emotions that might emerge. Finally, try to surmise what verbal or behavioral consequences might surface. Perhaps you or your family accepted some of these as well. I'll use the first pair of clichés as an example.

## Dr. Lynda L. Irons

You can't teach an old dog new tricks. (I'm old; therefore I can't learn anything new. This is a lie, self-curse, self-judgment and may also contain an implied vow. Emotions may be doomed, failure, useless, purposelessness, resentment, and more. This person may put himself down and choose not to try anything new.)

It's never too late to learn. (I must continue to learn or I won't measure up to expectations. This judgment will put pressure on this one to learn or else he may resort to rebellion against learning with a vow. He may feel pressured, stressed, angry, fearful, shameful, inadequate, rejected, and more. He may try to learn or he may refuse to try.)

Look before you leap.
He who hesitates is lost.

Out of sight; out of mind.
Absence makes the heart grow fonder.

Two heads are better than one.
If you want it done right, do it yourself.

Penny saved, penny earned.
Nothing ventured, nothing gained.

Opposites attract.
Birds of a feather flock together.

## Sticks and Stones

Haste makes waste.
Waste not, want not.

The nut doesn't fall far from the tree.

Anything worth doing is worth doing well.

Actions speak louder than words.

Rules are made to be broken.

Only the good die young.

*Like mother, like daughter.* Ezekiel 16:44.

You rise to the level of your incompetency and go no further.

Don't bite off more than you can chew.

There are many more that could probably be added to the list. Were you affected by any of them? Did you comply or rebel? What emotions are evident? Can you trace any discomfort to a particular memory?

Organizational Curses
Just as curses are often attached to individuals and families, there are also potential curses associated with organizations. We may incur curses, judgments, or other consequences for being joined

with an ungodly organization. We have previously noted that King David's administration suffered a famine because of the sin of his predecessor, King Saul. There are many church buildings that have been sold to a series of different congregations of different denominations and they each ended up with splits or having to sell the building because of dwindling membership. Coincidence or curse?

Consider connections to religious, political, social, business, military, educational, and other organizations like lodges, fraternities, sororities, or unions. We are warned not to be unequally yoked with unbelievers. We are linked in many ways to many groups, sometimes of necessity or by default. We are citizens of a country and state, members of a church, residents of some geographical area, belong to a fitness club, affiliated with a political party, and so on. Some organizations are fine, others may appear to be, but could have hidden events in their histories or charters which may be the cause of problems that are being experienced. Prayerfully research the history of those organizations to which you are linked.

Note: This author's book <u>What's in your Family Tree?</u> goes into more detail about this subject.

<u>Family Rules, Codes, and Values</u>

# Sticks and Stones

Spoken or unspoken family rules or codes of conduct determine values, mind-sets, expectations, and behavior. These rules are modeled and understood by family members. They are not written, but they may as well be posted on the refrigerator. Families often adopt clichés as a part of their value system.

Some of the verbal and non-verbal messages that dictate family attitudes and behavior about major issues deeply impact family members. Some children comply, others rebel. What did your family communicate verbally or by modeling regarding the following issues? Did your family lean toward the positive and encouraging side, or the negative and critical side? Does your family fall some place in the middle of the continuum?

Home is a safe, happy place or home is a dangerous, stressful place.
Identity is affirmed by behavior and activities or it is affirmed by character qualities.
Safety is found in association with others or in being independent.
Being sick or weak is a time to be shamed or a time to be pampered and cared for.
Success is defined by the world's standards or it is defined by God's standard.
Change is negative and scary or change is good and exciting.

In crisis, either we can make it through or this is a tragedy that will ruin us.

Children are valued as a blessing, or they are considered a nuisance.

An aunt wrote to her niece to affirm the niece's perceptions. "My Dutch upbringing gave me reason to feel shame about being sick or needing a doctor, and most always, I was told, 'it's all in your head.' I also received quiet messages that being sick and needing a doctor meant costing the family money, and this was another reason to feel guilty because for some reason we were brought up to think 'poor' – when in fact, it was simply a matter of family values – something so deeply imbedded within me that I still have to fight my way out of such ridiculous thinking! We are worth the very best! When we really believe this, we care for ourselves lovingly, and money or shame is nowhere in the picture."

The behavioral and emotional fallout from the people who were raised with some of the following family rules are included in the first half of the examples. Put your thinking cap on again and try to determine the fallout for the remainder of them. This is good practice for getting to the root of any possible issues with which you may also contend.

"Children are to be seen and not heard." An elderly gentleman, the youngest child, heard this as he grew up and continues to have difficulty in speaking up among other adults. This was compounded by his limited education. He perceived himself as being inferior and not having much of value to say.

"It's better to die than divorce." Ever since this woman was divorced by her husband, she continued to pursue him until she renounced this family rule that ruled her. Her mother repeated this rule often and especially at the time that the woman's marriage was crumbling. Shame and guilt hounded her. Once she was freed, she reflected on her behavior and said, "Oh, my, I must have driven him nuts after the divorce."

"Ladies (Christians) do not get angry." Many embrace these values. The Bible tells us to be angry, but not sin in the process. (Ephesians 4:26) Denying anger has led to other expressions of anger such as passive-aggressiveness, depression, and some diseases. (See this author's book on anger for more in-depth discussion.)

"There's a place for everything and everything must be in its place." This made for an orderly home. It was a good rule for a home in which one parent was legally blind. However, the children who were raised in this home were either perfectionists and nervous about clutter or rebelled against the rule with a vow. "I will not scrub my kitchen floor every Friday morning like Mom did!"

"You made your bed, now lie in it." There is very little forgiveness here for someone who may have made a mistake. Guilt, shame, abandonment, and rejection will surface in these family members who find themselves in a bad situation or a bad relationship after willfully or unknowingly making a decision that was subsequently destructive.

"Protect the family secrets." "Pretend everything is okay." "Don't air dirty laundry." "Appearances are everything." These are variations on a theme from several individuals. It leads to a very secretive, fearful life. Those who speak out are branded as traitors to the family and may be ostracized. They often feel guilty for seeking help and are frustrated by the limitations imposed by the rule.

"Something must be factual or provable by the scientific method to be valid." This family was dominated by an atheistic parent who was a scientist. Those who expressed faith in God were ridiculed.

"Be consistent." This family demanded consistency because it led to predictability and therefore control. There was much rigidity in thoughts and actions. There was reluctance to allow

## Sticks and Stones

for growth and maturity. Fear of being hypocritical arose when one desired to just change their mind about something as insignificant as choosing a new favorite color or flavor.

"Don't start one thing until you finish the last thing." Generally, this is a good idea; however there was rigid control in this family and guilt for those who violated the rule. Those who would naturally be able to multi-task were stifled. Creativity was suppressed.

"Stay with a job forever." The values of the older generation may have been beneficial and appropriate for them. Those who skipped from job to job were considered unstable and unreliable. The current generation does not have that stigma, but many suffer from the judgments of parents who held that value.

Use the following Family Rules as an exercise to hone skills for finding implied verbal assaults, the emotions attached, and possible behavioral and/or attitudinal issues.

"You better do it right the first time and every time."

"Agree or you're not accepted."

"If it takes up space, it better be useful. If it isn't functional, forget it."

"Resting or not working is a waste."

"Don't let your emotions show."

"If someone hurts you, cut them off."

"Eat it up, wear it out, make it do, or do without."

"Your father is the king of the castle, if he's wrong, he's still right. He makes the money and the rules."

"Work before play."

"Pull yourself up by your boot straps."

"Do a complete job or you get a partial allowance."

## Obverse or Mirror Statements

These verbal assaults form a negative implication based on a positive statement. It is the flip side of the coin. If the person does not live up to the positive, there will often be an implication that the negative is true. Many of the old sayings and family rules fit into this category as well. A number of people will also do this with Scripture verses.

"Cleanliness is next to godliness." This is not a Scripture verse, yet it is quoted as if it were. The implication is that those who are slobs are not godly. Think of all the people who are clutter bugs or have ADD or simply do not have housekeeping as their highest priority.

"God helps those who help themselves." Yes, we must make willful decisions to function in life, but this is not a Scriptural admonition and there are several implications. Most often, this is used as an indictment which is essentially a curse and/or a judgment against someone. A more accurate implied rendition might be, "I won't help you if I don't see that you are going to do something to help yourself."

"There but for the grace of God go I." The implication is that I am graced and you are not. You have fallen on hard times or difficult circumstances and I have not. Even though Christians do not believe in luck, it may also be translated, "You have bad luck and I don't."

*God loves a cheerful giver.* 2 Corinthians 9:7. I do not give cheerfully, therefore, God does not love me. This woman wrestled with complying with scripture by her actions as well as attitude and emotions. Since she struggled with giving cheerfully, she felt like a second-class Christian who was tolerated, at best, by God.

*For the eyes of the Lord are upon the righteous and His ears attend to their prayer but the face of the Lord is against those who do evil.* 1 Peter 3:11-12. Peter quotes Psalm 34:15-16. Therefore, I think God is against me and I must be evil because He is not attending to my prayers. Or, since I have done something evil, God is against me. Neglect, abandonment, inferiority, rejection, fear, and more flow from these thoughts.

<u>Superstitions</u>
Some are universal, others are religious, and still others are peculiar to regions or families. There are many, many superstitions that may not be recognized as such. They may be anything from an innocent "don't step on a crack or you'll break your mother's back" to a religious sign of the cross that falls short of a sincere gesture of faith to willful acceptance of an occult superstition.

The following are a few examples with some of the consequences that have been demonstrated in those who held them. Several more could probably be added to the list as well. Ask the Holy Spirit to help you discover anything that has crossed the line into superstition.

"It's bad luck to _____." Fill in the blank with walking under a ladder, crossing paths with a

## Sticks and Stones

black cat, or some other superstition. These may well give opening to demonic strongholds. Believing these deceptions may result in fears, phobias or erratic behavior.

"Every time I do/say/think/try _____, bad things happen." This may simply be an observation which holds much truth, but it may also cross the line into superstition.

"I have to go out the same door I came in or it is bad luck." A man would not go out the front door of a house he was visiting because he came in the back door. He judged the superstition to be true and that he would experience bad luck.

"Something will happen to my children because I had an abortion." This superstitious judgment was made by a woman who continued to feel the sting of guilt. She judged that she should be punished for her act by having her other children damaged. She judged that she was not permitted to enjoy her children.

"Knock on wood." This superstition came from the old Druid belief that demons inhabit trees and the wood that comes from them. By knocking on the wood, one would be able to make their statement without the demon hearing it, and thus, the demon would not be able to carry out the thing that is feared.

A woman asserted, "I didn't have my devotions that morning, that's why my daughter-in-law beat me up." Her well-being depended on her religious activities. It was essentially a superstitious activity to keep bad things from happening.

Song Lyrics
Many people embrace lyrics to a song, poem, hymn, Bible verse, etc. especially during times of distress. These may then become a combination of verbal assaults which rule their lives, especially the implied vows. Watch for lyrics that are embraced that could be the source of verbal assaults.

A depressed teenager who felt much rejection embraced Simon & Garfunkel's song, *I am a Rock*. Some of the lyrics reflect combinations of lies, vows, self-curses, and self-judgments. The lyrics declare that the person is alone, a rock, an island. The person has built impenetrable fortress walls because of painful relationships. He vows not to awaken feelings that hurt. He will turn to books and poetry to protect from failed love. He declares that he is shielded and safe by hiding in his room. His conclusion is that since a rock feels no pain and islands never cry therefore withdrawing from people, not allowing them to touch him, and not touching people will keep pain and crying away.

## Sticks and Stones

The teen who embraced these lyrics had been hurt in relationships and reacted with vows of isolation and self-protection. He had difficulties in building and maintaining relationships – including one with God – until the verbal assaults were dismantled.

Prayerfully ask the Holy Spirit to bring any song lyrics, poetry, or other similar items to mind. If there is a sense that something needs to be renounced, please refer to the prayer section at the end of this book for more help.

# 7
# RELEASE FROM VERBAL ASSAULTS

People come for biblical counseling and prayer ministry for a number of reasons. Some come because of distressing emotions. Some are conscious of disturbing thoughts that have plagued them for years. Others come to resolve a troubling situation. Still others come with vague complaints about a variety of issues that touch their lives and they are unclear about how to handle them. Some have mild and transient concerns; others have severe and life-dominating issues.

Regardless of the reason for seeking help, there are always verbal assaults involved. There is no set formula for finding verbal assaults and every person is different with a different set of verbal assaults and their accompanying emotions. Sometimes the emotions are readily apparent. Sometimes the thoughts are foremost.

## Sticks and Stones

There are principles and insights in this chapter that can give direction no matter what the presenting issue is. Even those who have overwhelming or life-dominating issues can use the principles and insights obtained from these concepts to gain a measure of relief.

It is much easier to pray with another person, but if a trusted person is not available, the Lord is faithful to meet the needy ones at His throne of grace. *For we do not have a high priest who cannot sympathize with our weaknesses, but One who has been tempted in all things as we are, yet without sin. Let us therefore draw near with confidence to the throne of grace, that we may receive mercy and may find grace to help in time of need.* Hebrews 4:15, 16.

It is a rare person who has a single issue that goes back to a single event. Praying with them is much like plucking a carrot. The entire plant is uprooted and it is finished. For most people, however, there are several events, verbal assaults, and other items that tie into the presenting problem. It is more like dealing with an octopus that has a number of tentacles. As each aspect is addressed, more and more freedom is experienced.

Remember that there can be one or many thoughts or verbalizations associated with issues and troubling situations. It is essential to understand that there will be a corresponding emotion associated with the thoughts and words. Emotions and thoughts will drive positive or negative behavior. When the thought, word, feeling, or negative behavior is recognized, a good place to start has been found.

Much of the book has explained and defined lies, vows, curses, and judgments. The examples included are written with the hope that they will trigger a reminder of a familiar verbal assault that may have been embraced. The categories of clues to detecting verbal assaults should also have helped.

Do not be distressed if it is difficult to clearly identify any of these things. God is faithful and He has provided His Holy Spirit. The Lord commands us to renew our minds. *And do not be conformed to this world, but be transformed by the renewing of your mind, that you may prove what the will of God is, that which is good and acceptable and perfect.* Romans 12:2. He will also provide the way for us to do so.

We have the mind of Christ, we need only to ask. *Now we have received, not the spirit of the world, but the Spirit who is from God, that we might know the things freely given to us by God, which things we also speak, not in words taught by human wisdom, but in those taught by the Spirit, combining spiritual thoughts with spiritual words.* 1 Corinthians 2:12.

# Sticks and Stones

Do not feel the need to be pressured to search your history to come up with the answer if it is not readily apparent. *The spirit of man is the lamp of the LORD, searching all the innermost parts of his being.* Proverbs 20:27. Relax and allow the Holy Spirit to do what He does best. The Holy Spirit can reveal to your spirit what is hidden in your heart and mind and brain.

It is most effective to have a series of short, directed prayers. The chain of prayers will follow whatever is revealed. For example, if a vow is recognized such as, "I must protect myself," you may have to wrestle with the reason for having made that vow. Then determine if you are willing to renounce that vow. Will you allow the Lord to be your protector? Must self-sufficiency be confessed? Is there someone involved that should be forgiven? Perhaps it will be necessary to go to the event which motivated you to make the vow in the first place.

The opening prayer may be something like this:

Holy Father, I come before Your throne of grace in the name of Jesus the Christ. You said that I could come to obtain grace and mercy in time of need. I have come with the desire to be set free from this issue that has encumbered me. I want to finish my race stronger than I started. Father, would You send Your Holy Spirit to stir in my mind and start me where You want me to start. Quicken the thought, word, emotion, issue, memory, or physical sensation to my mind so I can follow Your lead to the root of the problem. I ask these things in Jesus' name, amen.

Wait for a response. Sometimes it takes a few seconds, other times there seems to be a block. If nothing is sensed, ask the Lord to reveal the reason for the block. The most common answers to that prayer are:

- A verbal assault of some kind – "I don't think God will speak to me."
- Unforgiveness – "I can't forgive what he did, it ruined my whole life."
- Demonic interference – nausea, headache, dizziness, pressure, choking/gagging, mental block, bizarre thoughts, restlessness, inability to concentrate, altered senses, seizure, self-destructive impulses/behavior, or even a full demonic manifestation.
- Fear or other strong emotion in the event or relationship that has been avoided for so long – "I'm afraid to know who it was."

If it is <u>a verbal assault</u>, try one of these approaches: The first is to directly address it and renounce it with its stronghold and any associated demons. "Lord, I renounce the thought that You will not speak to me."

The second is to ask Jesus to address the verbal assault, "Jesus, You said that Truth will set us free. I have believed that You won't speak to me. What do You have to say to me about that belief?"

Another way is to ask the Lord to illuminate the root of that doubt. It may arise from an early memory in which a parent or other significant person would not listen to you or give an answer. There may be other implications, emotions, forgiveness issues, or other matters that the Lord brings up that must be addressed first.

If intense emotions begin to surface, ask the Lord to take you to the root of the emotions. "Lord, what is the root of *this* anger?" It may be the way an event was misinterpreted or processed. Do not feel pressured to search for the root; the Holy Spirit will bring it to mind. Ask Jesus to illuminate and bring further understanding.

Ask the who – what – where – when – why – how questions. "Lord, who spoke that over me?" "Lord, clarify what I am thinking." "Lord, where did I first encounter that?" "Lord, when did someone say that to me or when did that happen?" "Lord, why am I feeling that emotion?" Ask yourself how intensely that emotion feels and how true does that thought seem. It is helpful to rate the intensity of feelings and thoughts on a scale of 0 – 10.

<u>Unforgiveness</u> is a major block to hearing from God. If it is an unresolved forgiveness issue, there must be understanding about what Biblical forgiveness is and what it is not. Ask yourself if you are willing to choose to forgive the offender. Forgiveness is an act of the will. Peaceful emotions may or may not follow. Once forgiveness is granted, you will be able to proceed to resolving the verbal assault. (Please refer to this author's e-book, <u>Anger at God, Self, and Others</u> for a more complete explanation.)

If there is <u>demonic interference</u>, ask the Lord to reveal any so-called legal rights any demon may have to manifest in any way. When the source is determined and resolved, another verbal assault may need to be renounced. It is often a curse or judgment by a significant authority figure. A sin may need to be confessed and repented of, or perhaps some generational issue must be addressed.

When you know who you are in Christ and Whose you are, the battle is over. Know your identity! We have weapons to demolish strongholds according to 2 Corinthians 10:4. We defeat the enemy by the blood of the Lamb and the word of our testimony according to Revelation

12:11. We have been given authority to subdue demons according to Luke 10:17.

<u>Strong emotions</u>, especially fear of facing the issue, can be intimidating. Facing that issue will often require changes of some kind. The fears are often based on deceptions that have kept healing from being pursued for too long. "If I do not know, then my life won't change." "If I know that it was my uncle, then I have to face the fact that I let my little girl spend the night there." "I won't be able to have the same relationship with Mom anymore." "I don't want to know what really happened." "What if I made it up?" "What if I'm wrong?"

Ask this question: "What would happen if what I suspect *is* true?" Some things in life and certain relationships will inevitably change. There is a reluctance to rock the boat. Why stir things up now? And yet, you are unsettled until these issues are settled.

There are a great number of victims of early childhood trauma who question themselves. They try to dismiss it as coming from a wild imagination or something they read in a book, saw in a movie, or heard from someone else. They may try to downplay it: "It only happened once." "He did not mean it." "It was not that big a deal."

However, it really did have an impact on your life, your decisions, your relationships, and more. Once Jesus brings truth, fear dissipates, and you can move on to the root issue. Are you willing to trust God to walk you through your worst-case scenario; your worst fear?

# 8
# EMOTIONS AND BELIEFS

Emotions are just that: emotions. They are God-given tools to help us navigate life. They are there to help us detect injustice or danger or other sin-based issues. I have often said that emotions are great detectors – they let us know when there has been an injustice or that we should flee from a dangerous situation – but they are stupid. That's why God put them in our souls with the mind and the will so that we can think and choose. We do not want to be emotion-led people. We should strive to be Spirit-led people.

Emotions are fueled by the thoughts and beliefs that are embraced. The thoughts and beliefs, whether true or false, are reinforced by the emotions that are very real and feel very true. It can become a "catch 22" cycle. Identifying the emotion(s) and belief(s) is another key to healing as you ask God to identify the source of your issues.

## Dr. Lynda L. Irons

In a simple illustration of a common situation, you catch sight of a small, dark object that has legs coming from it; you immediately think that it is a spider. You pull back, your heart starts racing, and your body puts out adrenaline for the fight-or-flight response to this possible danger. After taking a second look, you realize the truth: it is merely a lint ball and there is no danger. You will calm down. Whether or not it was a real spider, there was an identical physical and emotional reaction.

In the same way, any event can be interpreted accurately or inaccurately. There will be an identical reaction to the event until it is determined whether or not the belief is true. A man believed all his life that his father wanted nothing to do with him after his parents divorced so he felt neglect, rejection, abandonment, anger, and more. When he became an adult, he found out that his grandmother was instrumental in keeping his father away. She intercepted phone calls and letters during the time he and his mother lived with his grandparents. She told his father that he was unwelcome and eventually he believed her and quit trying. Truth caused intense emotions to subside and be replaced by pity and compassion for a man who was denied his family.

A woman had worked through a memory about being abused, but there was still something unsettling within the memory. "Lord, what am I missing? What is still bothering me?" As she focused on the memory one more time, she found herself crying out, "Where was my mom?" The residual pain was not about the abuse, it was about feeling unprotected by her mother. As an adult, she knew that her mother was at home. The perpetrator had lured her into a shed. As a child, she had misinterpreted her mother's lack of protection. She felt deserted. This caused her to distrust her mother. The Lord brought an implied vow to remembrance – "I can't count on Mom." Once she had this realization, she quickly forgave her mother and renounced the vow. The pain in the memory was then completely healed, and she began to build a relationship with her mother.

Most of the time, pain in a memory comes from the presence of abuse, trauma, or other evil. Sometimes the pain comes from the absence of good things. In the example above, the little girl experienced both the pain of the abuse and the absence of protection.

The following section is intended as a tool to help identify the most common emotions and corresponding beliefs that are associated with them. Once the key emotion is known along with the accompanying belief, two essential components for dealing with your historical issues are handy. Some people do know exactly where the emotions and beliefs originated, but many do not.

Use the following emotions and beliefs to furnish possible specifics that are needed so the Lord can be asked to bring the root of the issue to mind. Many times the emotion listed in the main category adequately describes what is felt. If not, there are similar related words that may better help to pinpoint the feelings. Quite often healing comes more readily when the precise emotion is discovered.

After the emotion that best describes what is being felt is found, move to the corresponding thoughts and beliefs. Customize them to fit your specific situation as needed. Again, the thoughts originally embraced were intended for a narrow, limited situation regarding a specific person. However, the enemy is a legalist and a squatter and he will use these declarations to destroy.

For example, "I can't trust *anyone*" may have been directed at parents, but will include *everyone* – including God – even though that was not at all the intention of that person. He will wonder why he has a problem trusting God. It is not until he renounces that verbal assault that he will begin to break through in his relationship with God and people.

Most emotions will fall into the following main categories:

Abandonment, neglect, and rejection – These three emotions seem to run together. Whenever someone feels one of them, they are likely to also have issues with one or both of the others.

Anger and vengefulness – The Bible warns us to be angry, but not sin because of injustices. Unresolved anger is one of the primary reasons for blocks to healing. Vengeance belongs to the Lord.

Confusion – This emotion usually shows up when someone goes to an early childhood memory. A child does not have the mental capacity to process complex issues. Sometimes confusion occurs because of drug or alcohol use. Sometimes demons will be the cause of confusion.

Fear – This emotion may be what was felt in the memory or it may be fear of facing the memory. This is the emotion that should alert one about impending danger. It also drives other emotions, especially anger, hurt, and frustration.

Guilt and regret – Some will feel true guilt because they really did a bad thing. Others feel a false sense of guilt because of a situation for which they had no control. Regret comes from doing something that should not have been done or from neglecting to do something that should have been done.

Helplessness – This emotion comes from the belief that there may be a solution, but there is no way to attain it. There is a light at the end of the tunnel, but there is no getting there.

Hopelessness – This emotion, in contrast with helplessness, comes from the belief that there is no solution, no healing. There is no light at the end of the tunnel. There may not even be a tunnel.

Sadness, loss, and grief – These emotions come from actual losses, usually the death of someone close. They can also arise because of the loss of innocence, loss of an intact family, the absence of good, and so on.

Shame – This emotion comes from the humiliation that was endured. It is distinct from guilt and regret, although, sometimes shame will also arise alongside of those emotions.

Tainted – Most often, because of the demeaning nature of sexual sin, the person feels contaminated. Often this emotion will come along with guilt and/or shame feelings. Shame and taintedness need to be untangled for clarity.

Useless – This emotion comes from feeling that God and people would be better off without them. They cannot do anything right because they are defective. Suicidal thoughts often result.

In the following section, other words that fit into the above main categories are listed to better identify specific feelings. There are also the possible thoughts and beliefs that correspond to them that should be customized to reflect as precisely as possible what has been embraced either overtly or by implication. Some emotions will fall into more than one category.

For those who have no awareness of underlying emotions, it would be useful to begin with thoughts. Each person is different. Use the tool in whatever way it suits your situation best.

**Abandonment, neglect, and rejection**

Associated emotions: Disenfranchised, deserted, forgotten, discarded, left out, forsaken, displaced, lost, homeless, alone, betrayed, dumped, cast off, mistreated, ignored, overlooked, unseen, unwanted, second-hand, old, unwelcome, uninvited, orphaned, hurt, excluded.

Associated thoughts: "I don't matter." "No one cares about me." "No one protects me." "I can't trust anyone." "No one believes me." "They will leave and not come back." "I was a 'whoops' baby." "I have to take care of myself." "They care about my brother more." "I'm in the 'left-over' room." "I don't get taken seriously." "I'll control it so I get rejected on my terms."

## Anger and vengefulness

Associated emotions: Rage, fury, suicidal, homicidal, murderous, depressed, offensive, critical, sullen, competitive, confrontational, judgmental, bitter, strife, belligerence, hatred, defiance, combative, defensive, ill-tempered, hostility, seething, boiling, annoyed, irritated, antagonistic, resentful, incensed, exasperated, riled, cold, cruel, callous, justified.

Associated thoughts: "No fair!" "I am just so angry." "I want to hit him." "I want to make him hurt." "I could never forgive what was done." "I'll be vulnerable if I forgive." "I have a right to get even." "I cut to make myself feel better." "I can't let him get away with it." "I wish I was dead." "I cannot get over it." "She doesn't deserve forgiveness." "He should burn in hell." "I want to kill myself." "I have a right to hate him!"

## Confusion

Associated emotions: Bewildered, blind-sided, ambushed, dazed, perplexed, baffled, mystified, indecisive, dumb-founded, puzzled, disoriented, mixed-up, unsettled, at a loss, distressed, befuddled, stumped, uncertain, uneasy, doubtful, stuck, shocked, out of place.

Associated thoughts:  "I don't know what is happening." "Nothing makes sense." "Why would they do that?" "I don't understand." "What did I do wrong?" "I must be stupid." "I don't know what I can do to change things." "I feel stuck." "I don't know who I am supposed to be." "I just don't get it."

**Fear**

Associated emotions:  Scared, paranoid, nervous, agitated, doom, worry, desperation, ambushed, tense, dying, fearful, anxious, panic, terror, dread, apprehensive, alarmed, undecided, tentative, horror, trepidation, concerned, the creeps, foreboding, insecure, phobic.

Associated thoughts:  "I'm going to die." "I'm afraid of being a failure like Dad." "I'll be hurt." "Bad things will happen." "It's just a matter of time before it hits." "It's inevitable that it will happen again." "I'm not safe." "No one can protect me." "I'm doomed." "I don't trust God to override the devil's power." "I'll be hurt again." "I won't measure up." "This could kill me."

## Guilt and regret

<u>Associated emotions</u>: Rue, remorse, sorry, feel bad, repentant, lament, penitent, apologetic, disappointed, frustrated, condemnation, bemoan.

<u>Associated thoughts</u>: "Woulda/coulda/shoulda – didn't!" "It's my fault." "I deserved it." "It was because of my looks." "I'm a stupid idiot." "It felt good, so I'm bad." "I kept going back." "I started it." "I'll never live it down." "Everyone knows what I did." "I can't believe I did that." "I never wanted to be this kind of guy." "I feel bad that I hurt Mom and Dad." "I blame myself every day." "I could have stopped it." "If only…"

## Helplessness

<u>Associated emotions</u>: Trapped, cornered, intimated, defenseless, impaired, weak, powerless, incapacitated, choked, incapable, overwhelmed, impotent, frail, distressed, immobilized, feeble, vulnerable.

<u>Associated thoughts</u>: "I don't know what to do." "I can't do anything about it." "It's too much to handle." "They are too strong to resist." "God can't or won't help me." "I can't get out of this." "I have no resources." "I can never do anything right."

## Hopelessness

<u>Associated emotions</u>: Desperate, defeated, suicidal, impossible, doomed, bleak, condemned, fated, depressed, doubtful, destined, uncertain, disbelief, skeptical, hesitant, suspicious, having reservations, discouraged.

<u>Associated thoughts</u>: "There is no way out." "It will never get better." "Death is better." "I'll never amount to anything." "I have no other options." "What's the use?" "Nothing good will come of my life." "Quit now while I'm behind." "I can't figure it out by myself." "Why try?" "I will never catch up." "I don't measure up."

## Sadness, loss, and grief

<u>Associated emotions</u>: Regret, gutted, sorrow, grief-stricken, absence of good, isolated, alone, missing someone or something, undeserving, longing, traumatized, depressed, miserable, heartbroken, gloomy, despairing, despondent, hollow, melancholy, desolate, dejected, distraught, inconsolable.

<u>Associated thoughts</u>: "Dad had very little interest in my life." "Grandma was the only nice person I knew and now she's gone." "Mom was constantly disappointed in me." "I never really had a childhood." "I lost my virginity before

kindergarten." "I don't know if I can go on without him."

## Shame

<u>Associated emotions</u>: Ashamed, bad, corrupt, wrong, whore, sleazy, lazy, scandalous, fake, gross, failure, inept, foul, ignorant, gullible, indecent, dishonorable, ugly, unfit, nasty, sick, humiliated, embarrassment, disgraceful, disgusting, shunned.

<u>Associated thoughts</u>: "If I fail, I might as well indulge." "I felt disgust for myself." "I'm embarrassed that I would sink that low." "I was born out of wed-lock." "I don't fit in." "I fell off their pedestal." "I'm always trying to make up for my mistakes."

## Tainted

<u>Associated emotions</u>: Screwed up, nasty, disgusting, ruined, waste, flawed, loathsome, perverse, unclean, filthy, dirty, cursed, damned, faulty, defective, crazy, damaged, defiled, contaminated, spoiled, different, undesirable, stigmatized, inferior, inadequate, grimy, foul, polluted.

<u>Associated thoughts</u>: "I feel slimy because of what happened." "No one will really love me if they knew what he did to me." "I will always be damaged goods." "God won't be able to use me."

"Everyone can tell; they know there's something wrong with me."  "I felt so dirty."  "I am dirty because I allowed it to happen."

**Useless**

<u>Associated emotions</u>: Unappreciated, unacceptable, unsuitable, broken, disgrace, despised, outcast, inferior, worthless, belittled, unimportant, discounted, insignificant, irrelevant, invalid, no good, defective, faulty, imperfect, out of order, flawed, futile, pathetic, incompetent, inept.

<u>Associated thoughts</u>:  "I should never have been born."  "I can never please anyone."  "I'm not important." "I'm a burden, a mistake, a joke." "I'm not wanted or needed." "God could never use me." "I don't matter to anyone."  "I am worthless." "Should I even be here?"

Again, quite often a block is removed when a more precise feeling word is used or the verbal assault is more accurately stated.  Seeing the connection between emotions and thoughts should help in recognizing the link between some of your own thoughts and feelings.  The goal here is to help identify and confirm that which may have been denied or suppressed or suspected for a long time.

The more precise the prayer; the more specifically the Lord answers.  Approach His throne of grace and say, "Lord, this is what I am thinking and this is how it makes me feel. Where did this get started in my life?" He can then bring the hidden things to light and then something can be done about it. There are sample prayers in chapter ten to give practical language for praying about issues. Depending on the complexity of the issues, the help of a trusted friend, prayer minister, or Biblical counselor may need to be sought.

The following Scripture verses speak to issues which surround verbal assaults and becoming free. The Lord God truly wants everyone to be free of the encumbrances of the past. Some people say, "Just get over it." If that was possible, it would have been done a long time ago. Denial and suppression are also not a part of moving on. Old issues must be effectively dealt with once and for all in a biblical manner so that you can proceed unhindered and can finish the race stronger than it was started.

*THE SPIRIT OF THE LORD IS UPON ME, BECAUSE HE ANOINTED ME TO PREACH THE GOSPEL TO THE POOR, HE HAS SENT ME TO PROCLAIM RELEASE TO THE CAPTIVES, AND RECOVERY OF SIGHT TO THE BLIND, TO SET FREE THOSE WHO ARE DOWNTRODDEN ...* Luke 4:18.

*And do not be conformed to this world, but be transformed by the renewing of your mind, so that you*

## Sticks and Stones

*may prove what the will of God is, that which is good and acceptable and perfect.* Romans 12:2.

*We are destroying speculations and every lofty thing raised up against the knowledge of God, and we are taking every thought captive to the obedience of Christ.* 2 Corinthians 10:5.

*... and you shall know the truth, and the truth shall make you free.* John 8:32.

*If therefore the Son shall make you free, you shall be free indeed.* John 8:36.

*Jesus said to him, "I am the way, and the truth, and the life;"* John 14:6.

*And He who searches the hearts knows what the mind of the Spirit is, because He intercedes for the saints according to the will of God.* Romans 8:27.

# 9
# BLESSINGS

𝔄fter looking at the many negative verbal expressions, it is refreshing to take a brief look at blessings. *Like apples of gold in settings of silver is a word spoken in right circumstances.* Proverbs 25:11. *Pleasant words are a honeycomb, sweet to the soul and healing to the bones.* Proverbs 16:24.

Many of us have not been instructed in the amazing ministry of speaking blessings into our own or others' lives. The apostles spoke many blessings. It seemed to flow naturally in their greetings and benedictions. We would do well to declare and speak blessings over ourselves and others. James Goll said, "Greater is the power of the blessings than the power of the curse."

The ancient cultures incorporated blessings into significant life events. Patriarchs would gather the family by their death beds to bestow blessings upon their children. The Greek words for blessing mean several things: to speak well of, to praise, to cause to prosper, to make happy, and to celebrate with praises. It is the opposite of a curse.

The following are examples of blessings and benedictions that have been given in a variety of situations. There are specific blessings that can be prayed for others. Incorporate Scriptural blessings into prayers because in doing so, you have the privilege of agreeing with God as His words are repeated after Him.

*The LORD bless you, and keep you, the LORD make His face shine upon you and be gracious to you, the LORD lift up His countenance on you and give you peace.* Numbers 6:24 - 26. This was pronounced over the Israelites, but believers have been grafted in and enjoy this blessing.

Deuteronomy 28 explains the blessings of obedience. It would be worth reading the entire chapter. Blessings will come upon you and overtake you in the city, the country, your offspring, produce, basket, and kneading bowl. Blessings will be with your coming in and going out. Enemies will come in one way and be scattered seven ways. You will be the head and not the tail; above and not underneath.

*And all the people who were in the court, and the elders, said, "We are witnesses. May the LORD make the woman who is coming into your home like Rachel and Leah, both of whom built the house of Israel; and may you achieve wealth in Ephrathah and become famous in Bethlehem. Moreover, may your house be like the house of Perez whom Tamar bore to Judah, through the offspring which the LORD shall give you by this young woman."* Ruth 4:11, 12. Ruth became the great grandmother of King David and was in the lineage of Jesus Christ.

*Then Eli answered and said, "Go in peace; and may the God of Israel grant your petition that you have asked of Him."* 1 Samuel 1:17. Hannah was cursed with barrenness. Eli blessed her so she soon conceived and bore Samuel.

The king's servants came to bless David's son: *May your God make the name of Solomon better than your name and his throne greater than your throne!* 1 Kings 1:47. Solomon did expand the kingdom and was also a type of Christ.

*Now may the God of hope fill you with all joy and peace in believing, that you may abound in hope by the power of the Holy Spirit.* Romans 15:13.

*The grace of the Lord Jesus Christ, the love of God, and the fellowship of the Holy Spirit, be with you all. Amen.* 2 Corinthians 13:14.

## Sticks and Stones

*Peace be to the brethren, and love with faith, from God the Father and the Lord Jesus Christ. Grace be with all those who love our Lord Jesus Christ with incorruptible love.* Ephesians 6:23-24.

*Now may our God and Father Himself, and our Lord Jesus Christ, direct our way to you; and the Lord make you to increase and abound in love toward one another, and toward all men, even as we also do toward you; to the end that He may establish your hearts blameless in holiness before our God and Father, at the coming of our Lord Jesus with all His saints.* 1 Thessalonians 3:11-13.

*Now may the Lord of peace Himself continually grant you peace in every circumstance. The Lord be with you all!* 2 Thessalonians 3:16.

*The Lord Jesus Christ be with your spirit. Grace be with you. Amen.* 2 Timothy 4:22.

*Now may the God of peace, who brought up from the dead the great Shepherd of the sheep through the blood of the eternal covenant, even Jesus our Lord, equip you to do His will, working in us that which is pleasing in His sight, through Jesus Christ, to whom be the glory forever and ever. Amen.* Hebrews 13:20, 21.

*Grace, mercy, and peace will be with us, from God the Father, and from the Lord Jesus Christ, the Son of the Father, in truth and love.* 2 John 3.

## Dr. Lynda L. Irons

*Beloved, I pray that in all respects you may prosper and be in good health, just as your soul prospers.* 3 John 2.

The Bible is rich with blessings. Search them out and hide them in your heart so that in the day of trouble, the Holy Spirit can draw them out of the storehouse.

# 10
# SAMPLE PRAYERS

The following are a variety of sample prayers that are fairly comprehensive. They may need to be customized for your particular circumstances. They incorporate the principle of "put off" and "put on" that we see in the Scriptures. Pray big and let the Holy Spirit sort out the details. Be as specific as possible about people, situations, feelings, and verbal assaults.

Notice also that *active* verbs are used. For example, do not pray, "Lord, help me to forgive." Pray, "Lord, I confess that I have held a grudge and I choose to forgive as an act of my will." Use words such as "I choose," "I declare," "I repent," "I confess," "I renounce," "I rebuke," "I forgive," and so on.

When we put off or renounce or rebuke or repent or confess something, we must put on something else – forgiveness, the Holy Spirit, blessings, righteous declarations, truth, fruit of the Spirit, and so on.

Perhaps you are not a believer in Jesus Christ. It is possible that no one told you how to be born again or how to receive salvation. Maybe you have resisted the idea until now. Let me give a brief warning – Praying for the removal of demonic oppressors in someone who does not have the Holy Spirit to replace the eradicated unholy spirits brings the danger of becoming seven times worse according to Luke 11:24 – 26 and Matthew 12:43 - 45. *When the unclean spirit goes out of a man, it passes through waterless places seeking rest, and does not find it. Then it says, "I will return to my house from which I came." And when it comes, it finds it unoccupied, swept, and put in order. Then it goes, and takes along with it seven other spirits more wicked than itself, and they go in and live there; and the last state of that man becomes worse than the first.*

If you are not a believer, the things of God's kingdom cannot be put on. They are reserved for believers. The good news is that God wants everyone to come to Him so that He can take care of the sin nature that we were born with as well as each sin we have committed along the way and each sin that was committed against us.

## PRAYER FOR SALVATION

God, Your Word says in Romans 6:23, "*For the wages of sin is death, but the free gift of God is eternal life in Christ Jesus our Lord.*" I believe that You sent Jesus Christ to die for my sins and to give me a new nature. I now confess that I am a sinner by nature and I have committed many acts of sin by my words and my actions. Please cleanse me from all unrighteousness and fill me with Your Holy Spirit. I trust that You will lead and guide me in this new life with Christ. I pray this in the name of Jesus, amen.

## OPENING PRAYER

Heavenly Father, I come to Your throne of grace in the name of Jesus the Christ. Thank You that I can come here to obtain grace and mercy in my time of need. Father, Your word says that the spirit of a man is the lamp of the Lord and by it He examines the innermost chambers. I trust that You will take me to the root of the issue(s) that You want to heal today. I ask that You would clearly show me the thought, word, memory, issue, emotion, or physical sensation with which You want to start. Thank You for what You are about to do, amen.

# Dr. Lynda L. Irons

## FOLLOW-UP PRAYERS

There may be a loud and clear impression of where to start or things may be sensed more faintly. Something may come up which would be tempting to dismiss because it seems to have no bearing on anything. Let me encourage you to just go with it. If it proves to be a dead end or irrelevant, there is no harm. Just pray again. When you receive the answer to the opening prayer, your next prayer will probably be one of the following:

Lord, this is unclear and I am unsure. You are the light of the world. Would You illuminate this for me?

Lord, I am blank. I plead Your blood over any demonic plot to keep me from knowing the truth.

Lord, thank You for showing me this memory. What do You want me to see, hear, know, sense, or understand in it?

Lord, I am really feeling this emotion now. Where does <u>this</u> kind of (anger, fear, shame, etc.) come from?

Lord, I am reminded that I have said, _____. What is the root of this thought? (You may sense that it just needs to be renounced or that it needs to be traced to a deeper root issue.)

Lord, I see that I have been holding a grudge against _____. (See prayer for forgiveness below.)

Lord, I am feeling oppressed (pressure, nausea, tightness, headache, confused, etc.). Would You take me to the stronghold and root of that physical symptom if necessary? I renounce any demon afflicting me. (See prayer for deliverance below.)

Once there is a specific direction in which to go, use one or more of the following prayers that seem appropriate for whatever has been discovered. There may need to be a series of prayers because of the discovery of a variety of verbal assaults. Keep following the Lord's lead until the root is exposed, pray through it, and walk in freedom.

## PRAYER TO DISMANTLE LIES AND DECEPTIONS

God of all Truth, I believe _____. I have said or thought this most of my life. It feels very true yet my logic says that it contradicts the principles of Your Word. I ask that You would tell me what You think of that thought and bring me Truth that will set me free once and for all. I pray this in the name of Jesus who is the Way, the Truth, and the Life, amen.

Or

Father, I have believed _____. I choose now to declare what Your Word says about this. If it is necessary to go to the root of it, would You send Your Holy Spirit to lead me to that root so it can be eradicated once and for all. Amen.

PRAYER FOR HEALING OF INNER VOWS

Father, I bring before You an inner vow that I made over a situation that wounded me deeply. I confess that I essentially told You, whether consciously or subconsciously, what I would or would not put up with in the future. I have chosen to depend upon myself instead of You to keep me safe. In the name of Jesus Christ I hereby renounce the following vow as I consciously recall it: _____ as well as any implications which I believe were as follows: _____.

I ask Your Holy Spirit to go back through my history and render the words null and void, as if they had never been spoken or thought or acted upon for as many times as I spoke, thought, or acted. I plead the blood of Jesus over strongholds that have been established in me because of the vow(s) and any sinful behaviors or attitudes that flowed out of them. I ask that You would remove any and all demons who have been assigned to oppress me because of the strongholds established by my sin. In your grace and mercy, I ask that You would send them to a place where they will never afflict anyone ever again.

I ask that You would heal and seal all those broken places. Where there was darkness, bring Your light. Where there were curses, bring Your blessings, where there were lies and deceptions, bring Your truth which will set me free. I ask that the fruit of the Holy Spirit would flow out of that formerly wounded place: love, joy, peace, patience, kindness, goodness, faithfulness, gentleness, and self-control.

I also pray that You would do reciprocal healing in any others who may have been affected by these vows.

Thank You, Holy Spirit for interceding according to the will of the Father. Thank You for completing and correcting anything which may have been prayed incompletely or incorrectly. Thank You, Abba Father. Amen.

PRAYER AGAINST CURSES

Holy Father, I come before You having become aware that a curse has been directed at me. You have said in Your Word that a curse without cause shall not alight. I have experienced the effects of a curse. I ask that You would reveal the source of that curse if it is necessary for me to know. If not, I trust Your Holy Spirit to intercede according to Your will in this matter.

I now ask that Your Holy Spirit would render the curse null and void. I plead the blood of my Lord Jesus Christ over any strongholds that have been established as a result of that curse. Thank You for the *dunamis\** power of the Holy Spirit and the authority You have given to me. I further ask that You would command that any and all demons in the hierarchy who have been assigned to torment and oppress as a result of the curse and the stronghold be sent to a place where they will never be allowed to afflict anyone ever again. I pray that You would send reproaches back where they belong according to Your justice and mercy.

Now I ask that You would heal and seal these wounded places by the power of the Holy Spirit, I ask that You would fill the formerly dark places with Your light, replace all lies with Your Truth, and exchange curses with Your blessings. I ask that the fruit of the Holy Spirit would flow out of that place. I pray that You would allow the gifts of the Spirit to manifest without hindrance so that You will be glorified and Your will is done on earth as it is in Heaven.

I further ask that there would be a reciprocal work done in any affected family members, especially my children. You have also commanded us to bless those who curse us. I do now bless _____ despite the curse(s) directed at me.

Thank You, Holy Father for Your Word. You are holy and just. You are worthy to be praised. Amen.

\* *Dunamis* is the Greek New Testament from which we get our American word dynamite.

## PRAYER AGAINST JUDGMENTS

Righteous Judge, to You alone belong judgments. You are able to discern a person's heart. I confess that I have judged _____ for _____. By doing so, I have assumed the office of a judge. I have pronounced a verdict based upon my opinion of _____ and have had thoughts of condemnation towards him/her. I confess my sin.

Merciful Father, I pray that You will cleanse me from this unrighteousness. I pray that You will release me from the judgment that I have reaped by judging someone else. I pray that You would demolish the strongholds that have been created in my life because of this sin and ask that You would release me from any oppressing spirits.

Abba Father, I pray that You would pour your goodness upon _____. I pray Your richest blessings upon _____ and that You would do a work of reconciliation by breaking down any remaining barriers.

Thank You for Your grace and peace. I pray these things in the name of Jesus Christ. Amen.

PRAYER FOR WHEN YOU HAVE BEEN JUDGED

Father God, I am aware of having been judged. The judgment also served as a curse. I confess that I have also embraced that judgment/curse and gave it a place in my life by agreeing with the person who spoke it over me.

I now choose to renounce that judgment/curse that says _____ and I plead the blood of Jesus Christ over it. I ask that Your Holy Spirit would now render the words and the effects thereof null and void. I plead the blood of Jesus Christ over the stronghold(s) created by these words; and by the authority I have in Christ, I renounce and cast out the oppressing spirits that have plagued me. I ask You to go through my history and heal and seal every time and place where these words were spoken, thought, or acted upon. Fill those places with the presence of the Holy Spirit, the fruit of the Spirit, the blessing of the Truth, and Your judgments that You have for me regarding that old belief. Thank You for setting captives free! Amen.

# Sticks and Stones

## PRAYER OF REPENTANCE

Lord God, Your word clearly states that death and life are in the power of the tongue, that every careless word I speak will demand an accounting in the Day of Judgment, that I ought not bless You and curse a person who is made in Your image. I confess my sin and ask for Your cleansing from this unrighteousness. Set a guard, Oh Lord, over my mouth; keep watch over the door of my lips. Amen.

## PRAYER FOR FORGIVENESS

Father, I confess that I have held a grudge against _____ for saying/doing _____. Thank You that You have provided cleansing from all unrighteousness. I ask that You would demolish the strongholds and deliver me from oppressing spirits that have plagued me because of my sin of unforgiveness. Release me from any root of bitterness that brings defilement to myself and others.

I choose now, as an act of my will, to grant an unconditional grace to _____ that (s)he has not asked for and does not seem to deserve. Your Word says that vengeance belongs to You. I will stop trying to do Your job because righteousness and justice are the foundations of Your throne. I pray these things in the name of Jesus the Christ, amen.

(Refer to this author's work <u>Anger at God, Yourself, and Others – a Christian Path to Forgiveness, Reconciliation, and Trust</u> for more in-depth teaching.)

PRAYER FOR HEALING FROM ABUSE AND TRAUMA

Lord God, I am here at Your throne of grace to obtain mercy and grace regarding the abuse/trauma of _____ that I sustained earlier in my life. I recognize that it has caused me to think, feel, and behave in ways that are not pleasing to You or me. You are the same yesterday, today, and forever. I ask that You would go to my past and cover that trauma with the blood of Jesus the Christ and demolish every stronghold and remove every tormenting spirit that has oppressed me since that time. I ask that You would send those wicked spirits to a place where they will never afflict anyone ever again. Heal and seal this broken place with Your Holy Spirit.

I ask that You would also cover me from the top of my head to the soles of my feet with Your cleansing blood and healing balm. Bring peace and ease and soothing and comfort to every part of my body that was traumatized. I ask that You would heal any and all body memories associated with this trauma. I pray that You would correct and bring to balance any brain chemicals, adrenaline, hormones or any other natural human substance. I pray that You would heal every tissue, organ, or system that was affected by the abuse/trauma. Thank You that You make all things new. Thank You that You bring beauty for ashes. Thank You that no weapon formed against us will prosper.

I pray these things in the wonderful name of my Lord Jesus, amen.

PRAYER FOR HEALING OF SEXUAL ABUSE

Holy God and Father, I bring before You the sexual abuse (incest, molestation, rape) that I sustained earlier in my life. I feel tainted by this sin against me. I ask that You would cover that event with the cleansing blood of Jesus Christ. I ask that You would cut in two the cords of the wicked and release me from every direct and indirect unholy union, soul tie, and flesh link associated with that abuse.

I plead the blood of Jesus over every stronghold created by that abuse and I renounce and rebuke every foul spirit that has been given the so-called right to afflict me. I ask You to send them with their entire hierarchies to a place where they will never oppress anyone again. Please heal and seal this broken place by Your Holy Spirit and restore my purity and innocence. I ask for the healing of body memories and the healing of any damaged tissue as well. Thank You that You bring joy in the place of humiliation, taintedness, and shame. Thank You that You bring beauty for ashes. I pray this in Jesus' name, amen.

## PRAYER REGARDING SEXUAL SIN

Holy Father, I confess that I have sinned by _____ (fornication, adultery, pornography, lust, molestation, etc.). I know that Your Word says that if I confess my sin, You are faithful and just to forgive and cleanse me from all unrighteousness. Father, I ask that You would also cover me with the cleansing blood of Jesus and release me from the oppressing spirits and strongholds associated with the unholy unions, soul ties, and flesh links represented in those events. I pray for restoration of purity and holiness in my thoughts, words, and actions. I pray for reciprocal healing in anyone who was affected by my sin. I pray that You would release from any generational aspect and not allow future generations to be affected. I pray in the name of Jesus, amen.

## PRAYER FOR DELIVERANCE

Holy Father, I come to Your throne of grace in the name of Jesus the Christ. I ask that Your Holy Spirit would now occupy any place in or around me which has been occupied by any spirit which is now causing these symptoms (pressure, pain, queasy, headache, choking, etc.). You have given us authority to cast out demons in the name of Jesus. I plead Your blood over this area of my life. If it is necessary to address the so-called legal right of this demon, I ask that You would quicken that to my mind. I pray these things in the name of Jesus, amen.

Note: Any time a demon manifests in any way, it is no longer in its "assigned" place therefore it can be ousted by asking the Holy Spirit to fill that place. If the Lord takes you to a particular memory or thought, you may then have to forgive someone or renounce a verbal assault or address the issue(s) in the memory as well.

## PRAYER ABOUT HEAVENLY FATHER/EARTHLY FATHER

Abba Father, You created mankind in Your image as male and female. You intended for them to give their children a tangible image of You. Abba, we recognize that our parents have damaged that image by abandonment, lack of protection, lack of provision, lack of nurturing, and _____. Because of that, I realize that I have attributed the same flawed qualities to You. I confess that as sin and I ask that You would separate the image of my earthly father from my image of my heavenly Father. I ask that You would teach me to see You as

You are. Your word says that if my father or mother have forsaken me or let me down, that You would take me up. Father, they have let me down in some areas. I choose to forgive them for that. I ask that You would re-parent me – re-father me and re-mother me – in those areas where they failed. I bless them for all that they did well and I pray that as a parent, You would do reciprocal healing in this matter for my child(ren) since I was also not a perfect reflection of Your character. Thank You for Your grace and mercy, amen.

PRAYER OF BLESSING

*Now may the God of peace Himself sanctify you entirely; and may your spirit and soul and body be preserved complete, without blame at the coming of our Lord Jesus Christ.* 1 Thessalonians 5:23. I bless your spirit with clear communication with the Holy Spirit of God. I bless your spirit with being in its God-designed position over your soul and your body. I bless your spirit with hearing and responding to God so your spirit can communicate healing messages to your soul and body. I bless your soul with its mind, will, and emotions to be able to function in the ways God ordained – to respond to your world with appropriate feelings, to think with a renewed mind, to choose according to the will of God. I bless your soul to stay in alignment under your spirit and under the Holy Spirit. I bless your body as the temple of the Most High God. I bless your body with the blessing of Moses – his eye was not dim nor was his strength diminished when he died – that as your days, so also shall your strength be. I bless every system and cell of your body to be healthy and function according to the divine purposes God planned for each one. I bless you with favor in your home, community, church, and workplace. I bless you with joy. I bless you with gifts of the Holy Spirit and the fruit of the Spirit bubbling up in you all the days of your life. I bless you with Psalm 92:14 – that you will still yield fruit in old age. May the Lord bless you and keep you. May He cause His face to shine upon you and be gracious to you all the days of your life. Amen.

# 11
# FROM VERBAL ASSAULT TO TRUTH

𝔙ery few people have not spoken bleak or negative things about themselves or others. We do not often speak things that reflect our status as accepted citizens of God's kingdom. Confessions and declarations about identity should line up with the written Word of God. Ungodly thoughts must be transformed into godly declarations. We overcome the accuser because of the blood of the Lamb and the word of our testimonies. (Revelation 12:11) We do not want to walk in agreement with condemnation since that is the enemy's territory.

The following section lists several common verbal assaults. I have provided some Scriptures that counter them. This is not a formula. Ask the Holy Spirit to make the truth saturate your life. Ask Him to remove the lies and embed the truth deep into your being.

# Sticks and Stones

I will also challenge those who do not find a familiar verbal assault below to search the Scriptures for what the Lord has to say about particular thoughts that plague you. The prayers are short samples to give you a start. Customize them and find the most precise words that fit your situation.

<u>Verbal assaults</u>
"It is impossible." "It is too difficult." "It'll never work out."
<u>Truth</u>
*Ah, Lord GOD! Behold, You have made the heavens and the earth by Your great power and by Your outstretched arm! Nothing is too difficult for You,* Jeremiah 32: 17.

*Behold, I am the LORD, the God of all flesh; is anything too difficult for Me?* Jeremiah 32:27.

*But He said, "The things that are impossible with people are possible with God."* Luke 18:27.
<u>Turn it into a prayer</u>
Lord, I confess that I have believed that this is an impossible situation. Your Word says that it is possible with You. I choose to believe Your Word and will wait for Your solutions. Give me eyes to see and a mind to recognize Your answer to this prayer.

### Verbal assaults
"I'm too tired." "I am overwhelmed." "I'm so anxious all the time."
### Truth
*Come to Me, all who are weary and heavy-laden, and I will give you rest.* Matthew 11:28.

*Therefore humble yourselves under the mighty hand of God, that He may exalt you at the proper time, casting all your anxiety on Him, because He cares for you.* 1 Peter 5:6, 7.

*Rest in the LORD and wait patiently* (longingly) *for Him; fret not yourself because of him who prospers in his way, because of the man who carries out wicked schemes.* Psalm 37:7.
### Turn it into a prayer
Lord, I truly am weary from worrying about _____. I am coming to You and choose to rest in You. Every time I feel that anxiety and weariness, please nudge me by Your Holy Spirit to lay it down if I get wrapped up in it again.


### Verbal assaults
"Nobody really loves me." "I am unlovable." "My own parents don't even love me."
### Truth
*I have loved you with an everlasting love; therefore I have drawn you with lovingkindness.* Jeremiah 31:3.

# Sticks and Stones

*For God so loved the world, that He gave His only begotten Son, that whoever believes in Him shall not perish, but have eternal life.* John 3:16.

*A new commandment I give to you, that you love one another, even as I have loved you, that you love one another.* John 13:34.

<u>Turn it into a prayer</u>

Abba, Father, it feels so true that I am unlovable, even by You. I choose to believe Your Word and ask that You would bless me with not just knowing it in my head, but feeling it in my heart.

<u>Verbal assaults</u>

"I can't figure things out." "I just don't have what it takes."

<u>Truth</u>

*I can do all things through Him who strengthens me.* Philippians 4:13.

*Trust in the Lord with all your heart and do not lean on your own understanding.* Proverbs 3:5.

*But we have the mind of Christ.* 1 Corinthians 2:16.

<u>Turn it into a prayer</u>

Lord, I confess that I have tried to do it on my own and have excluded You. I do not have what it takes in my own mind, but I have Your Holy Spirit. I choose to trust You and believe Your word for a wonderfully creative solution at the right time.

### Verbal assaults

"I'm stupid." "I'm weak." "I'm a nobody." "I don't have what it takes."

### Truth

*... but God has chosen the foolish things of the world to shame the wise, and God has chosen the weak things of the world to shame the things which are strong, and the base things of the world and the despised, God has chosen, the things that are not, so that He might nullify the things that are, so that no man may boast before God.* 1 Corinthians 1:27-29.

*My grace is sufficient for you, for My power is perfected in weakness.* 2 Corinthians 12:9.

*"For I know the plans that I have for you,"* declares the LORD, *"plans for welfare and not for calamity to give you a future and a hope."* Jeremiah 29:11.

### Turn it into a prayer

God, it's hard to believe that You have chosen me when I seem to be so worthless. I confess that I have been trying to succeed according to the world's system rather than trying to please You. I ask for Your sufficient grace to let me see myself as You see me and to see that You do have plans and purposes for me.

## Sticks and Stones

<u>Verbal assaults</u>
"It's not worth it." "Why try?"
<u>Truth</u>
*For I consider that the sufferings of this present time are not worthy to be compared with the glory that is to be revealed to us.* Romans 8:18.

*... for momentary, light affliction is producing for us an eternal weight of glory far beyond all comparison ...* 2 Corinthians 4:17.

*Therefore, since we have so great a cloud of witnesses surrounding us, let us also lay aside every encumbrance, and the sin which so easily entangles us, and let us run with endurance the race that is set before us, fixing our eyes on Jesus, the author and perfecter of faith, who for the joy set before Him endured the cross, despising the shame, and has sat down at the right hand of the throne of God.* Hebrews 12:1, 2.

<u>Turn it into a prayer</u>
Oh, Lord, this trial is so difficult. I am feeling defeated and I want to give in. Would You bless me with Your perspective so that I can see the big picture and not be mired down in the daily grind?

Verbal assaults

"I just can't forgive myself." "I've done too much." "I'm irredeemable."

Truth

*If we confess our sins, He is faithful and righteous to forgive us our sins and to cleanse us from all unrighteousness.* 1 John 1:9.

*... who gave Himself for us to redeem us from every lawless deed, and to purify for Himself a people for His own possession, zealous for good deeds.* Titus 2:14.

*When you were dead in your transgressions and the uncircumcision of your flesh, He made you alive together with Him, having forgiven us all our transgressions, having canceled out the certificate of debt consisting of decrees against us, which was hostile to us; and He has taken it out of the way, having nailed it to the cross.* Colossians 2:13, 14.

Turn it into a prayer

Holy Father, I have so much guilt, shame, and regret for my actions. I know that I am instructed to forgive as You forgive. I choose to grant myself this undeserved grace. I am asking You to bless me with not just knowing that I am forgiven, but feeling the release as well.

## Sticks and Stones

<u>Verbal assaults</u>
"I can't manage." "I don't have the resources."
<u>Truth</u>
*And my God will supply all your needs according to His riches in glory in Christ Jesus.* Philippians 4:19.

*And God is able to make all grace abound to you, so that always having all sufficiency in everything, you may have an abundance for every good deed …* 2 Corinthians 9:8.
<u>Turn it into a prayer</u>
Jesus, You turned water into wine, You multiplied bread and fish. I confess my lack of faith to move this mountain of scarcity. I declare Your words that You will supply my needs and give sufficiency for this situation.


<u>Verbal assaults</u>
"I'm afraid." "I do panic and anxiety attacks."
<u>Truth</u>
*… casting all your anxiety on Him, because He cares for you.* 1 Peter 5:7.

*For God has not given us a spirit of timidity* (fear), *but of power and love and discipline* (sound judgment/safe thinking). 2 Timothy 1:7.

*The Lord is my light and my salvation whom shall I fear?* Psalm 27:1.
<u>Turn it into a prayer</u>
In the name of Jesus the Christ, I renounce a spirit of fear. I choose to walk in the security of my

Lord and Savior without fear. When the emotion comes up, I will turn to You each and every time. Thank You for caring for me.

Verbal assaults
"I'm agitated." "I can't settle down." "I can't stop thinking about it."
Truth
*Peace I leave with you; My peace I give You; not as the world gives do I give to you. Do not let your heart be troubled, nor let it be fearful.* John 14:27.

*Let the peace of Christ rule in your hearts ...* Colossians 3:15.

*Be anxious for nothing, but in everything by prayer and supplication with thanksgiving let your requests be made known to God. And the peace of God which surpasses all comprehension, will guard your hearts and your minds in Christ Jesus.* Philippians 4:6, 7

Turn it into a prayer
Jehovah Shalom, I come to You with all my agitation. I confess that I have been trying to do Your job by trying to control things or fix things. Teach me how to let the peace of Christ rule in my heart.

## Verbal assaults
"My life is a mess." "I'll never be able to figure a way out."
## Truth
*... we are afflicted in every way, but not crushed; perplexed, but not despairing...* 2 Corinthians 4:8.

*... for God is not a God of confusion but of peace ...* 1 Corinthians 14:33.
## Turn it into a prayer
Yes, Lord, I am perplexed. Thank You for your promise of clarity. Thank You for the examples of the saints who have modeled a godly attitude in confusing and painful situations. I will declare with them that I am not crushed and I will not despair in spite of natural circumstances. I will trust You to make a way of escape.


## Verbal assaults
"I'm all alone in this." "I have no one."
## Truth
*... for He Himself has said, "*I WILL NEVER DESERT YOU, NOR WILL I EVER FORSAKE YOU *..."* Hebrews 13:5.

*The* LORD *is the one who goes ahead of you; He will be with you. He will not fail you or forsake you. Do not fear or be dismayed.* Deuteronomy 31:8.
## Turn it into a prayer
Lord, You have chosen to repeat this many times in Your Word. I repent of excluding You from my

situation, not seeing or sensing You, and entrenching myself in solitude. Please bless me with being able to sense Your presence.

Verbal assaults
"It's useless; I will always be tempted." "I can't *not* do it."
Truth
*No temptation has overtaken you but such as is common to man, and God is faithful, who will not allow you to be tempted beyond what you are able, but with the temptation will provide the way of escape also, so that you will be able to endure it.* 1 Corinthians 10:13.

*... the Lord knows how to rescue the godly from temptation ...* 2 Peter 2:9.

*Since then we have a great high priest who has passed through the heavens, Jesus the Son of God, let us hold fast our confession. For we do not have a high priest who cannot sympathize with our weaknesses, but one who has been tempted in all things as we are, yet without sin.* Hebrews 4:14, 15.

Turn it into a prayer
Father, I feel like a prodigal who cannot return to You because I have not been able to have victory in this matter. I confess my sin once again. I renounce the stronghold and rebuke the oppressing spirits associated with it. I ask that Your Holy Spirit would heal and seal and fill me so that there is no more room for this in my life anymore.

# 12
# WEAPONS OF WARFARE

𝔚e participate with God in all matters of life by His design. He created us with free wills so that we may make choices. Those choices include proactively contending according to His will and guidance. We must not resign ourselves to a puppet-like existence and passively accept whatever comes our way. *For though we walk in the flesh, we do not war according to the flesh, for the weapons of our warfare are not of the flesh, but divinely powerful for the destruction of fortresses* (strongholds). *We are destroying speculations and every lofty thing raised up against the knowledge of God, and we are taking every thought captive to the obedience of Christ ... 2 Corinthians 10:3 - 5.*

The Bible has much to say about warfare. The purpose of the Old Testament books of the Bible are not merely to record the history of the Israelites. A deeper look will illustrate principles and insights into spiritual warfare. The Lord gave Moses and

Joshua specific instructions for each battle. Sometimes they led with Judah – which means praise – and sometimes they led with the Levites. Sometimes they set an ambush. Sometimes they just stood and watched the Lord annihilate their enemy. There was no set strategy. They followed His lead.

So too, we must be sensitive to the leading of the Lord and His Holy Spirit whenever we encounter conflict. Jesus warned His disciples that there would be conflict in the world, but they should not fret because He has overcome the world. Allow the Lord to direct which of the following weapons should be drawn from your spiritual arsenal and the timing of its use. Willfully choose to be engaged in spite of physical weakness or emotional fatigue.

**The Word of God** – When God's Words are repeated in prayers and in warfare, there is a greater impact than uninspired words that come from the flesh. David had to war in the natural realm so we could war in the spiritual realm. The Psalms contain many warfare themes.

*In the beginning was the Word, and the Word was with God, and the Word was God.* John 1:1.

*All Scripture is inspired by God and profitable for teaching, for reproof, for correction, for training in righteousness; that the man of God may be adequate, equipped for every good work.* 2 Timothy 3:16, 17.

# Sticks and Stones

**Praise** – The enemy hates praise. He flees from its presence. Break out your hymnal or listen to praise and worship music.

*Let the high praises of God be in their mouth, and a two-edged sword in their hand.* Psalm 149:6.

*Yet You are holy, O You who are enthroned upon the praises of Israel.* Psalm 22:3.

*Through Him then, let us continually offer up a sacrifice of praise to God, that is, the fruit of lips that give thanks to His name.* Hebrews 13:15.

**Prayer** – Pray for God's will to be done on earth as it is in heaven. In heaven, there is no turmoil or sickness or pain. His ears are attentive to your cries. Colin Smith said, "Prayer is how God's promises are delivered." Our prayers fill the heavenly bowls and flow back to earth when they are filled to overflowing with both our prayers and God's.

*Another angel came and stood at the altar, holding a golden censer; and much incense was given to him, so that he might add it to the prayers of all the saints on the golden altar which was before the throne. And the smoke of the incense, with the prayers of the saints, went up before God out of the angel's hand.* Revelation 8:3, 4.

*Pray without ceasing.* 1 Thessalonians 5:17.

*Now He was telling them a parable to show that at all times they ought to pray and not to lose heart ...* Luke 18:1.

**Plead the blood of Jesus** – The enemy does not like to be reminded that the blood sacrifice of Jesus defeated him.

*... but if we walk in the Light as He Himself is in the Light, we have fellowship with one another, and the blood of Jesus His Son cleanses us from all sin.* 1 John 1:7.

*When He had disarmed the rulers and authorities, He made a public display of them, having triumphed over them through Him.* Colossians 2:15.

*Then I heard a loud voice in heaven, saying, "Now the salvation, and the power, and the kingdom of our God and the authority of His Christ have come, for the accuser of our brethren has been thrown down, he who accuses them before our God day and night. And they overcame him because of the blood of the Lamb and because of the word of their testimony, and they did not love their life even when faced with death."* Revelation 12:10, 11.

**Communion** – We often think of this as a corporate sacrament, but there are times when private communion is acceptable and necessary to battle against oppression. Again, the enemy does not want to be reminded of his defeat. This sacrament is closely tied with the blood of Jesus.

*... Jesus took some bread, and after a blessing, He broke it and gave it to the disciples, and said, "Take, eat; this is My body." And He took a cup and gave thanks, and gave it to them, saying, "Drink from it, all of you; for this is My blood of the covenant, which is to be shed on behalf of many for forgiveness of sins.* Matthew 25:26 – 28.

# Sticks and Stones

*For as often as you eat this bread and drink the cup, you proclaim the Lord's death until He comes.* 1 Corinthians 11:26.

**Declare your testimony** – There is power in a testimony. Make declarations that affirm that you are standing firm with the Lord.

*The LORD is my light and my salvation; whom shall I fear? The LORD is the defense of my life; whom shall I dread?* Psalm 27:1.

*For this reason I also suffer these things, but I am not ashamed; for I know whom I have believed and I am convinced that He is able to guard what I have entrusted to Him until that day.* 2 Timothy 1:12.

*For I am convinced that neither death, nor life, nor angels, nor principalities, nor things present, nor things to come, nor powers, nor height, nor depth, nor any other created thing, shall be able to separate us from the love of God, which is in Christ Jesus our Lord.* Romans 8:38, 39.

**Anger and Forgiveness Issues** – If there is anger because of a sin against you, confess it and forgive the offender. This is a proactive way to defeat the enemy if unforgiveness remains toward any offender. He will have no leverage to oppress you.

*BE ANGRY, AND YET DO NOT SIN; do not let the sun go down on your anger, and do not give the devil an opportunity* (stronghold). *Let all bitterness and wrath and anger and clamor and slander be put away from you, along with all malice. Be kind to one another, tender-*

*hearted, forgiving each other, just as God in Christ also has forgiven you.* Ephesians 4:26, 27, 31, 32.

*Then the Lord said to Cain, "Why are you angry? And why has your countenance fallen? If you do well, will not your countenance be lifted up? And if you do not do well, sin is crouching at the door; and its desire is for you, but you must master it."* Genesis 4: 6, 7.

The anger was the result of Cain bringing an unsuitable offering to God. He knew God's required sacrifice, but it angered Cain to have the offering rejected. God gave Cain a choice to master the sin or to allow the sin to master him. He chose badly. Do not go the way of Cain.

**Unity** – There are many true sayings about unity. There is safety in numbers. United we stand; divided we fall. One mule can pull nine hundred pounds, but two mules can pull three times that amount. When God's people are all of one mind, there is a mysterious strength that comes from that synergy.

*Only conduct yourselves in a manner worthy of the gospel of Christ; so that whether I come and see you or remain absent, I may hear of you that you are standing firm in one spirit, with one mind striving together for the faith of the gospel; in no way alarmed by your opponents – which is a sign of destruction for them, but of salvation for you, and that too, from God.* Philippians 1:27, 28.

*Again I say to you, that if two of you agree on earth about anything that they may ask, it shall be done for them by My Father who is in heaven. For where two or three have gathered together in My name, there I am in their midst.* Matthew 18:19, 20.

*Behold, how good and how pleasant it is for brothers to dwell together in unity! ... for there the* LORD *commanded the blessing – life forever.* Psalm 133:1, 3.

*There is one body and one Spirit, just as also you were called in one hope of your calling; one Lord, one faith, one baptism, one God and Father of all who is over all and through all and in all.* Ephesians 4:4 – 6.

**Put off/Put on** – There are many tangible and intangible non-Christian items and/or experiences that are to be put off and replaced by things and values of the Kingdom of God. If the old is not replaced with the new, there will be a continued battle for victory in any area that is tainted by sin. The new cannot be added to or blended in with the old.

*And He was also telling them a parable: "No one tears a piece from a new garment and puts it on an old garment; otherwise he will both tear the new, and the piece from the new will not match the old. And no one puts new wine into old wineskins; otherwise the new wine will burst the skins, and it will be spilled out, and the skins will be ruined. But new wine must be put into fresh wineskins.* Luke 5:36 – 38.

*Do not lie to one another, since you laid aside the old self with its evil practices, and have put on the new self who is being renewed to a true knowledge according to the image of the One who created him.* Colossians 3:9, 10.

*... lay aside the old self, which is being corrupted in accordance with the lusts of deceit, and that you be renewed in the spirit of your mind, and put on the new self, which in the likeness of God has been created in righteousness and holiness of the truth.* Ephesians 4:22 – 24

**Armor of God** – In the familiar passage in Ephesians 6:10 - 17 we are admonished to put on the full armor of God so that we may be able to stand firm against the schemes of the devil and resist in the evil day. We are to have our loins girded with truth, to put on the breastplate of righteousness, have our feet shod with the preparation of the gospel of peace and take up the shield of faith. We are to put on the helmet of salvation and take up the sword of the Spirit – the word of God.

Some people semi-superstitiously go through the physical motions of putting on the armor every morning. Others do this as a meaningful tangible reminder. But it begs the question, "How does one lose their armor? Does it evaporate overnight?"

If I embrace lies and deceptions, faulty judgments and other verbal assaults, I will no longer be girded with truth. If I think or behave in an unrighteous manner, there will be holes blown into the breastplate of righteousness. If I walk in chaos and confusion, my feet will no longer be shod with the preparation of the gospel of peace. If I live

## Sticks and Stones

with doubt and do not embrace the promises, the yeses and amens of God, then my shield of faith is compromised. If I deny or doubt my salvation, I will have removed my helmet of salvation. If I do not saturate my life with the word of God, I will have dropped the only offensive weapon I have at my disposal.

If we are admonished to put the armor on by an act of obedience, then we may also willfully choose to put it off. Do not lay down any of your weapons of warfare lest the enemy take advantage.

Dr. Lynda L. Irons

# CONCLUDING REMARKS

It is my hope and prayer that the principles taught in this small volume on the basics of combating verbal assaults would be effective tools to free the captives, the down-trodden, and the broken-hearted. I wandered in that wilderness for far too many years myself. I believed far too many lies, processed life events inaccurately, made harmful vows, and embraced curses and judgments. There were very few blessings pronounced over my life.

I grew up in a time when people who sought counseling were stigmatized. There were very few biblical counselors available. Unfortunately, many of them "Christianized" their secular training. Dr. Phil was not even on the scene. Trauma, especially sexual trauma, remained hidden in the closets of the victims' minds.

After I received much healing, I made a vow. My vow – a beneficial vow – went something like this:

## Sticks and Stones

"No one was there for me, so I will be there for them so that they don't have to take decades to find healing like I did."

I am grateful for the truths that I was able to glean from so many wonderful teachers, conference speakers, and authors over the decades in my search for freedom through truth. There is no way that I could list all of them, but among them are: Focus on the Family's Counselor Enrichment Program, Ed Smith's Theophostic basic and advanced training, Aiko Hormon's healing conference, Neal Lozano's Unbound, Cleansing Streams, Hawkin's Restoring Shattered Lives, Neil T. Anderson's Freedom in Christ, John and Paula Sandford's Elijah House, Randy Clark's School of healing and deliverance, Arthur Burk's Plumbline Ministries, IFOC's Chaplain training, Freelandia Bible College and Seminary, and more. Each one has contributed to the body of knowledge that accumulated within me over the years.

The requests to share these principles led to individual, marital, and family counseling as well as seminars and conferences that I was invited to present. The seminar materials were the skeletons upon which this and the other counseling-related books were fleshed out. Several of the counseling related books listed below will go into greater depth for issues that were mentioned briefly in this book.

Dr. Lynda L. Irons

## BOOKS BY DR. LYNDA L. IRONS

Counseling related e-books (watch for upcoming paperback editions)

Anxiety and Panic Attacks – Help from a Christian Perspective
Seeing, Hearing, Sensing God Through His Brokenhearted Children
I am a CUTTER, Please Help Me – Help from a Christian Perspective
Yo soy un Cortador Ayúdame, Por favor (Spanish edition of I am a CUTTER)
Angry at God, Yourself, and Others – a Christian Path to Forgiveness, Reconciliation, and Trust
Eating Disorders – Help from a Christian Perspective – Anorexia Nervosa and Health Food Obsession, Bulimia Nervosa and Binge Eating
Heaven or Hell – Have I Lost My Salvation?
Spiritual Gifts – Discovering Your Spiritual Gifts
What's in Your Family Tree?
Dissociative Identity Disorder – Basics from a Christian Perspective

Fiction – available in e-book or paperback

Ritual Abuse – Autumn
Ritual Abuse – Winter
Ritual Abuse – Spring
Ritual Abuse – Summer

www.ingramcontent.com/pod-product-compliance
Lightning Source LLC
Chambersburg PA
CBHW061943070426
42450CB00007BA/1036